SHORT CUTS

INTRODUCTIONS TO FILM STUDIES

SHORT CUTS

INTRODUCTIONS TO FILM STUDIES

FOR A COMPLETE LIST OF TITLES IN THE SERIES, PLEASE SEE PAGES 143–44

THE STARDOM FILM

CREATING THE HOLLYWOOD FAIRY TALE

KAREN McNALLY

WALLFLOWER

NEW YORK

Wallflower Press is an imprint of Columbia University Press.
Columbia University Press
Publishers Since 1893
New York   Chichester, West Sussex
cup.columbia.edu

Library of Congress Cataloging-in-Publication Data

Names: McNally, Karen, 1964– author.
Title: The stardom film : creating the Hollywood fairy tale / Karen McNally.
Description: New York : Wallflower Press, [2020] | Series: Short cuts | Includes
   bibliographical references and index.
Identifiers: LCCN 2020019027 (print) | LCCN 2020019028 (ebook) | ISBN 9780231184014
   (paperback) | ISBN 9780231851145 (ebook)
Subjects: LCSH: Fame in motion pictures. | Fame on television. | Fame—Social aspects—
   United States.
Classification: LCC PN1995.9.F347 M36 2020 (print) | LCC PN1995.9.F347 (ebook) |
   DDC 791.43/65—dc23
LC record available at https://lccn.loc.gov/2020019027
LC ebook record available at https://lccn.loc.gov/2020019028

Columbia University Press books are printed on permanent and durable acid-free paper.
Printed in the United States of America

Cover image: cineclassico / Alamy Stock Photo

In memory of Lena and Eddie McNally

CONTENTS

ACKNOWLEDGMENTS

My thanks go to my editors at Columbia University Press, Yoram Allon for commissioning this book, and Ryan Groendyk for his guidance and for making the editing process such a smooth experience. I am also grateful to Kathryn Jorge and the wonderful production team who saw this book through to publication. Huge thanks go to Steven Cohan, whose encouragement of the project throughout its development and comments on early versions of the chapters have been invaluable. Feedback from the anonymous reviewers of the manuscript was similarly both reassuringly generous and helpful, and I am most appreciative of their time. I am also indebted to various schools at London Metropolitan University for funding research trips that have resulted in this book, and to the staff at the Margaret Herrick Library of the Academy of Motion Picture Arts and Sciences for their invaluable assistance as I conducted this research.

THE STARDOM FILM

INTRODUCTION

In the 2011 film *The Artist* (dir. Michel Hazanavicius), George Valentin, Jean Dujardin's Hollywood movie star of the silent era, suffers a career and personal crisis at the arrival of sound pictures. As a swashbuckling, charming, Douglas Fairbanks–style action star, he dismisses the coming of sound and fails to recognize until it occurs that this new technology will turn him into an outdated irrelevance to America's movie audiences. While fans once cheered for Valentin onscreen, laughed at his skits onstage with his co-star terrier, and clamored for him as he hammed it up outside theatres, the changing industry and evolving audience tastes leave the star broke, unemployable, and on the brink of suicide. The fan he meets cute after a premiere—Peppy Miller, played by Bérénice Bejo—simultaneously takes advantage of instant press attention to make a play for stardom, moving from an extra in a silent movie to the chorus of a musical, supporting roles, and eventually the moniker of "Hollywood's new sweetheart" as the leading lady of the talkies. The film's resolution comes in the restoration of Valentin's stardom through a combination of the romantic attraction between the two stars and the silent movie star's embrace of Hollywood's future, played out in a musical production number in the genre that initiated sound cinema.

The Artist won five Oscars at the 2012 Academy Awards—including for Best Motion Picture—and, as a European production, illustrated the global appeal of Hollywood movie history and, more particularly, the potency of the mythology surrounding stardom. The footprints of earlier American stardom films litter *The Artist*, from the two Hollywood star versions of *A Star Is Born* (William A. Wellman, 1937; George Cukor, 1954), to Peppy's name play on Marion Davies's Peggy Pepper/Patricia Pepoire in *Show People* (King Vidor, 1928), to the star's transition from silent to sound movies through the musical in *Singin' in the Rain* (Gene Kelly and Stanley Donen, 1952). In turn, *The Artist* itself functions as a reference point for the contemporary renewal of the stardom narrative in the 2016 musical *La La Land* (Damien Chazelle). As both films draw on the imagery of glittering stars that frames the "Beguine the Beguine" number, danced by Fred Astaire and Eleanor Powell in 1940's *Broadway Melody of 1940* (Norman Taurog), *La La Land* continues the visualization of romanticized stardom that their narratives, and those of their predecessors, similarly display.

Screen narratives concerned with stardom reach into the history of Hollywood filmmaking as far back as the pre-studio era and have seen something of a revival in recent years, both in film and on television. Scholarly consideration of these films collectively, however, has previously failed to emerge despite some groundbreaking work located around either more focused or, alternatively, overarching topics. The exploration of a select series of films within this genre, for example, is illustrated by Lucy Fischer's and Shelley Stamp's takes on the gendering of stardom through silent film narratives centered on the "movie-struck girl,"[1] or J. E. Smyth's discussion of 1930s examples as a form of Hollywood historicizing.[2] More regularly, stardom narratives have been examined amid what Steven Cohan, in his exceptional 2019 book *Hollywood by Hollywood*, has termed "the backstudio picture."[3] Cohan's comprehensive historical and critical study of Hollywood movies that dramatize Hollywood filmmaking, alongside the specific themes of Christopher Ames's *Movies About the Movies*,[4] as well as the variously detailed overviews of these films, all explore narratives about Hollywood stardom within a wider framework of films about Hollywood.[5]

Stardom narratives, however, form an extensive yet distinct category in Hollywood's history, a self-reflective treatise on the most central element of the industry and its films: Hollywood's stars and the mythology through which their stardom is constructed. As Cohan argues for the backstudio picture, the conventions of formal structures or studio definitions are far from the only means of signifying genre. Genres might additionally be defined by audience and critical reception, occur retrospectively, or take form through a continuity established across several decades of film history.[6] While colliding with conventional genres in the framework of Hollywood's acknowledged genre hybridity, the stardom film is therefore discussed in this book as a genre retrospectively defined and formed across Hollywood film and television history through recognizable narrative tropes and themes.

This book thus sets out to both define a previously unrecognized genre and explore its representation, promotion, and mythification of stardom, tracing the genre's history from its beginnings to the present day. My choice of the term "stardom film" identifies the concept of stardom as the central theme addressed by these films and articulated through its star characters. While the narratives of backstudio films might be constructed around a variety of topics related to filmmaking and the film industry (with protagonists ranging from directors and producers to stars and adjacent figures), the stardom film is fundamentally concerned with dramatizing stardom through star characters, with its core meta-theme that of stardom itself. Similarly, films centering on international movie stardom, or categorized as European or world cinema productions (such as the aforementioned *The Artist*), or those that examine other forms of stardom—in music or sports, for example—might certainly be explored within the broader boundaries of the genre of the stardom film. However, this book frames the genre around American-produced films that feature Hollywood movie stardom as their essential concern. Only television breaches these borders, both as a medium that produces relevant films and in the narrative depiction of star careers, which historically have moved between these two entertainment fields since America's postwar era. As *Once Upon a Time . . . in Hollywood* (Quentin Tarantino, 2019) suggests, however, Hollywood movie stardom remains in the cultural imagination as its ultimate form, surpassing television and international film stardom, just as the film defines its protagonist by his confinement to the latter.

The narratives within this genre as it is explored throughout this book therefore settle centrally around defining Hollywood movie stardom, depicting the strategies employed by Hollywood to discover, brand, and promote the individuals through whom it might be expressed, even as permanence remains elusive, and showing its constant lure for audiences and for those who seek to claim the title of Hollywood star. Through the films' characters, narratives display the experience of stardom as they negotiate the dynamic between star and studio; attempt to win, maintain, and regain their status; and battle the threats of scandal, age, or audience disaffection. In doing so—and whether wholly or partly fictionalized, or a shadowy combination of real and fictional movie stars—the characters represent stardom as both career and desire, born, made, lived, and lost in its mythological homeland of Hollywood.

The star characters in these films therefore become the embodiment of the desirability of Hollywood's heightened brand of stardom, conveying through the narrative a mythology that retains its potency throughout the genre's history. The essential myth of the Hollywood star as a figure "at once ordinary and extraordinary, available for desire and unattainable"[7] positions the star in an unparalleled imaginary as a modern American version of the gods and goddesses of Greek mythology, captivating audiences on- and off-screen and as an emblem of both divinity and mortality.[8] As Michael Williams describes this seemingly unattainable yet defining state: "They can be held up to the heavens but never quite belong there."[9] The films of this genre play out these contradictions in ways that repeatedly reinforce star mythology as this contemporary fairy tale is realized in narrative and visual form. Star characters are therefore glamorous yet down-to-earth workers transformed for the delight of admiring audiences; narratives show stars being discovered as if they were Lana Turner acting out her own myth at Schwab's drugstore, before the charisma that makes such discovery inevitable becomes identifiable on the screen; and their natural possession of star quality suggests stars that are born, while the industry strategies that the films display suggest stardom is also very much made. Characters express a desire for stardom, become objects of worship, and attempt to remain figures of identification as ideal stars, while themselves remaining worshippers of the myth of stardom, tied to the impact of its history on their present, layering further the genre's construction and reinforcement of star mythology. Stardom as a concept and the retelling of its myths are the genre's ultimate concern.

Following the release of William Wellman's *A Star Is Born* in 1937, *New York Times* critic Frank Nugent, who would later be nominated for an Academy Award as screenwriter of John Ford's *The Quiet Man* (1952), compared the spate of films about Hollywood to a striptease, explaining that "in the very best strip tease tradition, it [Hollywood] has been seeking to preserve the glamorous illusion; always it has flounced offstage with protective hands over the greatest of its mysteries."[10] The backstudio element of stardom films, like the broader collection of films to which they belong, has frequently offered a critique of the mythology through which stardom is constructed, often by exposing the problematic industry–star–audience dynamic in which the narratives' star characters exist. As Nugent suggests, however, resolution comes just as readily in the restoration of the star myth upon which these stories rest. The overwhelming of critique through a reestablishment of star mythology is further supported by the framing of stardom narratives within the larger myth of Hollywood. The shift in location for American filmmaking from New York and New Jersey to Los Angeles in the first decade of the twentieth century enabled the founding of Hollywood as what Kevin Starr describes as "a town, an industry, a state of mind, a self-actualizing myth."[11] Tied geographically and symbolically to the narrative of adventure inherent in California's mid-nineteenth-century Gold Rush, America's movie business was transformed into the nation's most potent modern myth of imaginable possibilities. Central to the myth was the movie star, on display in Hollywood's surroundings and representing a realization of the dream audiences saw on-screen.[12] The gradual democratization and gendering of fame, combined with the studios' targeting of female audiences, made movie stardom particularly appealing to women seeking their own land of opportunity,[13] instilling the stardom narrative with a feminine and disruptive essence that remains in contemporary examples of the genre despite any shifts in industry attention toward male stars and audiences. The historical lack of racial diversity in the genre's representation of stardom, in turn, both reaffirms the whiteness of the industry's definition and prompts the stardom narrative's most unambiguous disturbance to stardom mythology in contemporary examples of, in particular, the star biopic, a theme taken up further in this book's afterword as it considers depictions of African-American stardom.

Since Hollywood's fascination with stardom has prompted the production of stardom narratives in large numbers from the 1910s to the 2010s, this abridged study of the subject makes no attempt to be comprehensive. While covering this extensive history of filmmaking, the aim of this book is to explore key films that illuminate the core areas discussed regarding the stardom film and illustrate the compelling force of star mythology. The history of the genre that unfolds, and its narrative association of star mythology primarily with female stardom, means that a majority of the films discussed illustrate this focus. In the same way, the omission of particular films has largely been the result of either limitations of word length or the broader Hollywood focus of those films. Vincente Minnelli's duo of films concerned with filmmaking, for example, have not been included for both of these reasons. In a larger study, *The Bad and the Beautiful* (1952) and *Two Weeks in Another Town* (1962) would have found some space, but a primary focus on the producer and director figure, respectively, excludes them from my analysis here. Similarly, while worthy of more scholarly attention than it has so far received, *Hollywoodland*'s (Allen Coulter, 2006) shifting narrative focus to a detective story in its Hollywood setting leaves this title for consideration elsewhere. The alternative emphases in these excluded films revolving around male protagonists again points to the genre's insistence on female stardom as the embodiment of its mythology. Few of the early short films have been examined due to a focus on feature-length movies, including the silent avant-garde critique *The Life and Death of 9413: A Hollywood Extra* (Robert Florey and Slavko Vorkapich, 1928). In addition, both the association of particular stars with the stardom genre and the impact of star imagery on narratives and characterization necessarily run through this study. One regrettable star omission, therefore, is Doris Day and her early films with Warner Bros., which establish the active ambition that becomes part of her screen identity. The development of Day's image in relation to stardom, alongside the heightened self-reflexivity and mythmaking in *My Dream Is Yours* (Michael Curtiz, 1949) and *It's a Great Feeling* (David Butler, 1949), means that Day's star image deserves further consideration within the specific context of the stardom film genre than it is able to receive here.

While the main chapters in this book take a thematic, rather than an historical, approach, the study explores films across the twentieth and twenty-first centuries. Moreover, just as a historical framework is explicitly applied where particular issues arise through representation or production, the sequence in which the chapters' themes are addressed creates a historical narrative that is in itself illuminating. As the films and television biopics of recent decades forcefully indicate in chapter 3, therefore, the maintenance and reinforcement of the mythology of stardom increasingly becomes the genre's primary concern. The chapters consider the essential notion of mythology in the stardom film both narratively and through various forms of representation. In the first chapter, "Core Stardom Narratives," the essential narratives of the stardom film are outlined and explored, as they establish key tropes for the films of the genre. Chapter 2, "Genre and Hybridity," considers the ways in which defined studio genres impact the stardom narrative. Examining the musical, melodrama, film noir, and horror in the context of various avenues of hybridity, this chapter explores the effects of genre on the types of narrative developed and the ways in which star mythology is represented. Chapter 3, "Character, Star, and Myth," examines the blurred boundaries between the "real" and fictional worlds, which becomes central to the stardom film's dramatization of the star myth. Exploring the impact of star images on both character and narrative, and considering fictional and fact-based films, as well as their overlapping spaces, the final chapter examines how the essential combination of myth and reality plays out in a multitude of ways and lies at the heart of Hollywood's endless attachment to the stardom narrative. The book concludes with an afterword that looks at the whiteness of the stardom film genre, considering existing narratives that explore racially and ethnically defined stardom and positing areas for development in the stardom film within a shifting cultural and consequently industrial landscape.

1   CORE STARDOM NARRATIVES

The new Western mythology that swiftly developed around Hollywood as a site of limitless possibilities—embodied in the success, fame, and glamour of the movie star—was consolidated by narratives that depicted the literal and figurative journey to stardom. Early stardom films through to those of the 1930s established the alignment of mostly female characters' ambitions with an escape from the traditional religious and gendered spheres of control existing in their rural family homes. The appeal of stories of stardom to female audiences who identified with the characters' boundary-breaking adventures initiated a self-fulfilling process as young women descended on Hollywood in search of similar fortune. Studios actively promoted a transformational link between fandom and stardom, enabling women to imagine themselves within the same scenarios they viewed in the films. Female fans were therefore specifically targeted with advice in the mid-1910s on how to best ensure silver-screen success, as the studios encouraged them to try their luck in the dream factories. The heady mix of mythology and direct encouragement combined with stark warnings to the "movie-struck girl" of what it took to succeed.[1] In the 1924 book *The Truth About the Movies by the Stars*, Norma Talmadge was one in a lineup of movie stars detailing the daily grind of moviemaking and slim chances of success; she reassured hopefuls that "perhaps, again, some director may 'discover' her. He will call her from the back ranks into the foreground close to the camera. Then will come her opportunity. If she has been well trained, if she uses her brains; if she rises to the occasion success will follow."[2]

The reassertion of mythology amid ambivalent warnings about the fickleness of fame combines here with an emphasis on the myths of discovery and charisma as only part of the foundation for the realization of stardom. With the addition of training, smarts, and determination, Talmadge suggests, the motivated young girl "will" secure stardom. This blend of mythology, alongside tropes of hard work and active aspiration, forms a key element of narratives in which the protagonist's need to escape is transformed into a desire for stardom and those that articulate a definition of the model star. Just as prospective stars are warned of the dangers of scandal to their careers, the achievement of stardom comes with lessons on how it might be maintained. Films make clear that stars need to fulfill their requirements as professionals, not only as workers within the studio system but also in order to retain an essential relationship with the audience on whom their stardom is reliant. Frequently depicted as fans-turned-movie stars, those who veer from a combination of ordinary and extraordinary, of hardworking and glamorous (and in doing so threaten to disrupt the stardom myth) are assured of various forms of failure in the studios, with their audience, and in their personal lives.

The model star and the disruptive star, often presented as the film's contrasting versions of stardom, both serve to reassert core mythology and become the central framework of the rise-and-fall narrative. The depiction of female professional desire, hard work, and success within Hollywood's studio system when set against male personal and professional decline becomes the most potent articulation of the mythological roadmap to achieving and maintaining stardom, as well as pointing to the inevitable results of its rejection. These key narratives structured around ideas of stardom as an escape, of the model star, and of the rise and fall of stardom form core themes established in films from the 1910s to the 1930s and play out persistently across the genre as the stardom film negotiates its celebration of stardom's triumph with reassertions of its limits.

Escaping to Stardom

The idea of Hollywood stardom as an escape features prominently in early silent examples of the stardom film. Notably emphasizing female escape from limitations or control, these narratives are constructed less around ambition than happenstance, as their characters find themselves by chance transported into the world of moviemaking. The films frequently set up a rural-urban divide, drawing on the cultural and moral rifts evident in moves toward the Prohibition era, which was established after the ratification of the Eighteenth Amendment in 1919 and remained in force until its repeal in 1933. This action to amend the U.S. Constitution followed continuous resistance against reforms proposed by religious and other pressure groups in cities like New York and Los Angeles that had set the scene for speakeasies and organized crime. Hollywood therefore becomes a modern oasis in stark contrast to the restrictive past, from which these characters secure their escape. In the 1913 Mack Sennett comedy short *Mabel's Dramatic Career*, for example, Mabel Normand runs away from a fickle suitor (played by Sennett) and life on the farm, only to happen upon a film crew, become a star, marry her co-star, and start a family. When her jealous suitor discovers her success and points his gun toward the idyllic domestic scene he spies through her window, a bucket of water from above is the film's comedic commentary on a violent rural attempt to disturb what stardom has enabled.

A Girl's Folly (Maurice Tourneur, 1917) draws directly on industry concerns about the "movie-struck girl," warning America's young women about the sophisticated lifestyle of Los Angeles and that stardom is reserved for the few. In rural New Jersey, Mary (played by Doris Kenyon) dreams of a troubadour while declaring to her local marriage option, "I could never be happy as a farmer's wife." When she by chance comes across a crew filming a western, the Hollywood adventure and the movie star she meets (played by Robert Warwick) seem the incarnation of her romantic dreams of an escape. The screen test—which will repeatedly appear in the genre—reveals Mary's lack of screen presence, asserting charisma as an essential component of movie stardom and leading this country girl into what the film depicts as an immoral relationship with her film star lover. When her mother returns Mary to her rural home, country suitor, and future as "a farmer's wife," the narrative suggests that this girl's folly was not to believe in a romanticized Hollywood dream, but instead was the attempt to realize herself without foundation as the embodiment of the Hollywood myth.

In the comedy *Ella Cinders* (Alfred E. Green, 1926) starring Colleen Moore, Hollywood becomes the fairy-tale escape route from an abusive family when the modern-day Cinderella wins a contest to star in a movie. Although the studio is revealed as phony, Ella's determination to become a movie star leads to success, a long-term contract, and Ella becoming the toast of her town after she wanders onto a film set and is this time officially discovered. The narrative simultaneously allows her small-town sweetheart to escape his wealthy father's traditional perspective on the class divide, with a conclusion that settles the movie star, the ice truck owner, and their new child in the democratic terrain of Hollywood.

The depiction of Hollywood stardom as an attainable myth bringing success and a contented family life to the hardworking young woman with the requisite charisma defines the budding star and her goal in clear terms. These films, in making escape their central narrative theme, present stardom as the modern woman's entrée into the new world, provided she has the tools and talent to negotiate her way around this city on a hill. Both chance and an ultimate desire play their part, but for the "movie-struck girl" to become a star, she must actively seek an escape from the restrictions of the past and take a leap into a world of possibilities.

Goldwyn's melodrama *Souls for Sale* (Rupert Hughes, 1923) takes these ideas further in a narrative that draws implicitly on the context of the country's growing rural-urban divisions grounded in religious and cultural differences, which play out through their impact on establishment attitudes toward Hollywood. The film more directly references the increasing pressure on the studios in light of a number of real-life scandals, including the infamous 1921 Roscoe "Fatty" Arbuckle legal case, which followed the death of Virginia Rappe at a Hollywood party, and the unsolved murder of actor and director William Desmond Taylor in 1922. The studios heads attempted to quell political and religious outrage and resist external censorship by forming the Motion Picture Producers and Distributors of America (MPPDA) in 1922 headed by ex–postmaster general Will Hays, while continuing to provide audiences with the kind of entertainment they desired. This Hollywood resolve is part of the background, into which the film launches its protagonist.

Souls for Sale was something of a one-man production for director Rupert Hughes, who adapted his own novel for the screen and produced the film for Goldwyn. *Exhibitors Herald*, an early version of the trade magazine *Motion Picture Herald*, ran an abridged serialization of the novel across several issues in 1923. In his foreword, Hughes made plain his target of regressive religious moralizing and his unashamed aim to restore the image of Hollywood and its stars:

> In "Souls for Sale", I have tried first of all to tell a story of moving picture life; second, to make it true to its life; and third, to give a true idea of the life outside. And so I take a minister's daughter for my heroine, and I show that she has no end of temptation and misfortune in her snug (and smug) little home town. She finds in the moving pictures first a refuge, and then a fascinating life-work.[3]

In Hughes's story, immorality is born not in modern cities but in the "smug" religious confines of middle America. As evidence of censorship's influence, Hughes reveals his decision to not commence the film's narrative with a storyline of his protagonist's illegitimate pregnancy, which "was not even criticized when published in magazine and book form and later in the newspapers. But to make any use of it at all on the screen, would violate the rules of every censor board, and set the axes to swinging."[4]

Goldwyn's promotional strategies for the film were aimed at both reversing societal views of Hollywood as a den of immorality and promoting stardom as a legitimate career choice. In April 1923, the *Exhibitors Herald* reported that the studio was tying marketing of the film into a larger national campaign utilizing civic organizations, the Los Angeles Chamber of Commerce, and film actors to "broadcast the truth about Hollywood," noting, "Sincerity is expected to banish the mirage of sin that scandal evoked west of the Great American desert."[5] Stardom as an achievable goal was repeatedly evoked through marketing strategies that included "camera test" stunts, audience members competing on stage in impersonations of actors, daily success stories about getting into the movies, and questionnaires in which fans detailed their qualifications for stardom and their ideal roles.[6] Such strategies aimed to blur the lines between Hollywood and its audience, neutralizing the negative impact of the scandals and reasserting the myth of stardom as a realizable dream.

Souls for Sale itself similarly presents Hollywood as a community of workers battling the morality judgments of small-town America's religious zealots who meanwhile enable the killing spree of a mass murderer. Its melodramatic plotline centers on Remember "Mem" Steddon (played by Eleanor Boardman in her first starring role), a young woman from a rural background escaping a pastor father who preaches the evils of Hollywood from the pulpit, and a new husband later revealed as a serial killer who murders women for their insurance money. The film's focus, however, is stardom, accentuated by the title cards that introduce each of the lead actors at their first appearance on screen.

Mem's wedding night flight from her husband from the back of a train initiates the escape that will become her path to stardom. The mythologi cal status of Hollywood is introduced when Mem finds herself in the desert and happens upon a Rudolph Valentino–like scene of star Tom Holby (played by Frank Mayo) seated atop a camel. This chance encounter introduces Hollywood stardom as a possible refuge—a symbolic oasis—from patriarchal control identified through both violence and religious hypocrisy. When she asks, "Are you real or a mirage?," Holby's response—"Neither; I'm a movie actor"—places the mythological star somewhere between reality and fantasy (figure 1.1). This is the moment of Mem's

Fig. 1.1: *Souls for Sale* (Goldwyn Pictures, 1923). Mem (played by Eleanor Boardman) is introduced to Hollywood as an oasis and stardom as a myth after escaping patriarchal control.

13

discovery, occurring by chance and yet wholly justified by the success which follows. Mem's hard work and perfection of a craft are set against her father's religious intolerance of the secular culture Hollywood represents and a husband whose sexual jealousy leads him to pursue her across countries. When Mem's husband tries to reclaim his wife and condemn Mem for her artificial lifestyle, the star fights back, asserting the work ethic of her profession and her personal independence: "I don't belong to you—or anybody. I belong to myself."

The film depicts Hollywood throughout as a working community, as Mem initially wanders through scenes with Charlie Chaplin, Erich von Stroheim, and ZaSu Pitts, and later becomes the hardworking star of the screen who answers her own fan mail and rises at dawn for a day of filming. *Souls for Sale* refutes Hollywood's morally corrupt image, representing the industry conversely as a guardian of probity and warning Mem as a newcomer of the perils of scandal. For example, she observes an agent rejecting an offer from an actress to "pay the price" to secure a role because "it's the public you've got to sell yourself to—not to us!" Mem is also schooled by director and eventual love interest Frank Claymore (played by Richard Dix) on the injustices of scandal when he advises, "When an actor gets into trouble, they blame the screen. A scandal is fatal to any one in the moving pictures."

While these moments work alongside the representation of heroine Mem and her journey to stardom to signal Hughes's admitted mission of countering prevailing ideas of a depraved industry, an article in *Screenland* suggests the scenes were, more importantly, part of the film's knowing use of clichés, bonding director and audience in a shared perspective: "We can fairly see Rupert Hughes winking at us individually, confidentially."[7] The offer of marriage that Mem finally accepts from Claymore provides the narrative's ultimate prize for her daring rejection of religious and patriarchal control. When the director promises Mem, "I'll build your soul to its height—and sell it for you to the world, if you'll let me," the film suggests that a future consisting of creative partnerships and international stardom should be every woman's dream—and might feasibly be their reality. After a melodramatic finale, during which Mem's husband is killed in his attempt to murder Claymore and a fire rages on the set while the director continues filming, the film reasserts Hollywood's professional identity and service to its audience in the final title card: "They are only players, after

all; but they mean well and work hard, spinning pictures for the amuse-
ment of strangers. And they can never know, until it is too late to change,
whether their toil will win them censure or applause."

Escaping from Stardom

Films repeatedly promoted Hollywood stardom as an achievable career
goal for the American (often) woman with the requisite work ethic and
screen presence, rescuing them from the controls and restrictions embodied in small-town, rural life. Yet the latter also intermittently served to provide a contrasting escape narrative, allowing movie star characters some
respite from the pressures of the filmmaking capital and locating them in
what to the successful star now exists as an alternative world of everyday
Americans. The desire to escape was frequently the extent of the films'
commentary on Hollywood, however, with the sojourn in the wilderness
always temporary and critiques of the star phenomenon from locals being
forcefully rejected, usually by the stars themselves. The narratives instead
represented an additional means of reinforcing both the core relationship
between stars and the Hollywood studio system and the myth of stars'
ultimate difference, drawing the characters back to the dream factory by
the final reel as the other world again became the location from which to
escape.

In the 1935 film *In Person* (William A. Seiter), Ginger Rogers plays
movie star Carol Corliss, scared into an agoraphobic state by persistent
adoration from her fans. When her psychiatrist convinces a stranger
(played by George Brent) to allow her to accompany him to his mountain
retreat, his task is to reconnect her with her pre-Hollywood self, thereby
curing her condition. Corliss resists, however, his dismissal of stardom as
the "great American myth," countering, "I like being a myth," and is cured,
in fact, when the local cinema screens one of her films, allowing her to
reconnect with her fans. His co-option into the mythology is complete
when the director on her film set refers to him as "Mr Corliss."

Mae West's comedy *Go West Young Man* (Henry Hathaway, 1936)—a
title playing on West's name, as well as explicitly linking past and present
myths of the West—introduces her as a movie star tiring of the controls on
her love life inflicted by her Public Relations Manager (played by Warren
William), and a studio contract that prevents her from marrying for five

years. When her Rolls Royce breaks down en route to a personal appearance and forbidden assignation with a politician, her stay at a bed and breakfast in the country offers an unintended escape from moral restrictions and press intrusion. The film suggests the blurred lines of morality between the two worlds, hinting—as a narrative ruse—at impropriety and an "illegitimate" pregnancy among the moral superiority of rural America and positioning the Hollywood studios as guardians of their stars' moral welfare. While West combines sexual enticement of a local gas station owner, played by Randolph Scott, with the lure of a Hollywood movie career, mostly older locals disparage the business for its artificiality and express consternation at West's behavior on- and off-screen. The film makes clear, however, the reach of Hollywood's appeal, showing most of the inhabitants enraptured by West's arrival, most notably the bed and breakfast's young maid, who has a bedroom wall covered with movie star publicity shots, practices poses in her hand mirror, and attempts an impromptu audition for the Public Relations Manager with an impersonation of Marlene Dietrich (figure 1.2). Even Scott's naïve mechanic has been working on a Hollywood sound system. The narrative concludes, therefore, with dissenters in the thrall of stardom's glamour as they imagine themselves as movie stars, and West and William returning to Hollywood in a romantic union symbolizing Hollywood's triumph over both its sexually unruly star and rural America's lingering traditional values.

The 1933 screwball comedy *Bombshell*, directed by Victor Fleming and starring Jean Harlow, presents a more ambiguous take on both Hollywood and stardom in its frenetic depiction of a movie star fleeing the chaos of a life over which she has minimal control. While family and household staff take advantage of the lifestyle provided financially by Lola Burns, publicity agent "Space" Hanlon (played by Lee Tracy) constructs an identity for Lola as the studio's "Hollywood Bombshell," has a suitor arrested and threatened with deportation, stymies his star's attempt to adopt a child, and hires a troupe of actors to ensure her speedy return to Hollywood. Straddling the pre-Code censorship timeline in 1933, the narrative hints at a sexually free lifestyle for Lola through past relationships with Hanlon and director Jim Brogan (played by Pat O'Brien), suggesting her attempts to confront Hollywood control, even as the studio exploits her image to sell everything from movies to perfume and stockings. Yet the film presents Lola's identity as a series of performances, from the blonde bombshell of

Fig. 1.2: Americans are captivated by movie stardom as Mae West's star escapes Hollywood in *Go West Young Man* (Paramount, 1936).

"men, scrapes, dazzling clothes, a gorgeous pin wheel personality," as Hanlon convinces her the audience desires her, to a counterimage as a domestic goddess, to the prospective mother of an adopted child—prompted by an interview with *Ladies' Home Companion*—and a traditional romantic ready to relinquish stardom for marriage. As Brogan comments on her purported desire for marriage and motherhood: "You're playing a scene with yourself. I'd like to have a camera turned on you right now. Say, you'd be a sensation."

Lola as text is reinforced by the film's referencing of Harlow's screen image with a scene showing Lola on the set of *Red Dust* (Victor Fleming), Harlow's 1932 film with Clark Gable, and Fleming doing retakes of the barrel scene, as well as an excerpt of the two stars in an on-screen kiss during the opening montage. This is in addition to the character being modeled on Clara Bow since the story's conception as a stage drama that never reached production. Fleming's professional and romantic relationships with Bow prompted his insistence that the comedic screen version continue to draw on Bow's life and image,[8] apparent in Hanlon's reference to Lola as the "It Girl." Even Lola's escape to a desert spa, having tired of continuous publicity stunts and studio control, becomes an attempt to perform the role of an ordinary American, an image hampered by her arrival in the company of her personal maid Loretta (Louise Beavers) and three Old English sheepdogs. When she falls for Franchot Tone's fake high-toned poet, and he and the actors posing as his family express their disapproval of movie stars, Lola reverts to her star identity, pointing to the relationship between stars and their audience in defense of Hollywood: "Those people are my friends. Why, they sent me presents and wrote me all their troubles." Indeed, as she makes her case against pomposity and we learn Tone and his "family" are actors in a set-up staged by Hanlon, performance itself becomes the point. Their performed manipulation of Lola serves to restore her to her identity as a star, pushing her to an impassioned defense of Hollywood and stardom, proclaiming, "What's wrong with pictures? It's perfectly honest work, isn't it? More work than those clinkers ever did. Is it any disgrace entertaining people, making them laugh and making them cry?" Once again, Hollywood reasserts itself when Lola scrambles to return to the studio to prevent a rival actress from poaching her title role in *Alice in Wonderland*, and a blossoming romantic relationship between star and publicity agent suggests the ideal professional union.

Modeling Stardom

As the recurring theme of escape illustrates, the ways in which these films define stardom draw essentially on the updated Western mythology circulating around Hollywood as a land of opportunity and the notion of the star as both ordinary and extraordinary, displaying their difference while remaining fundamentally tied to the Hollywood audience. The characters are often first defined as fans of the silver screen themselves, which initiates their path to stardom, and find evidence of their impact as stars when they escape the geographical confines of Hollywood. This acknowledgment of the core relationship between stars and the audience frequently becomes the means through which narrative equilibrium is negotiated, restoring protagonists to their role as stars and, moreover, as protectors of Hollywood's reputation. Reinforcing the myth of the ideal star therefore becomes a key feature of the stardom film and the focus of a number of early narratives.

King Vidor's 1928 silent comedy *Show People*, reportedly modeled after Gloria Swanson's career,[9] starred Marion Davies as Peggy Pepper, a Hollywood hopeful who achieves major success as the star of a string of melodramas, while actor and Peggy's sweetheart Billy Boone, played by William Haines, languishes on the second rung of the slapstick comedies through which Peggy got her break. Peggy's arrival in Hollywood with her father is depicted as that of the movie-struck girl, dazzled by the location and excitedly spying John Gilbert outside the gates of MGM. On her way to success, however, she notably fails to recognize many of the stars who litter the film, such as Charlie Chaplin, who requests her autograph following her first film premiere, or, in a moment of explicit self-reflexivity, Marion Davies as herself on the studio lot. When she abandons slapstick for the melodramas she views as "real *art!*," such as Vidor's *Bardelys the Magnificent* (1926), which is previewed after her own film, her perception of a clash between art and entertainment signals her problematic detachment from the audience. Peggy's subsequent name change to Patricia Pepoire, her relationship with her co-star, an ex-waiter now calling himself Andre d'Bergerac, le Comte d'Avignon (played by Paul Ralli), the interview she gives to Louella Parsons on a chaise longue, and her insistence on a string ensemble accompanying her arrival on set all reinforces the image of a star straying far from the ideal.

The film's use of genre is central to this imagery and made evident specifically when Billy disrupts Peggy's intended wedding to Andre by spraying her with seltzer and throwing a pie in the groom's face (figure 1.3). The physicality of slapstick is necessarily a rebuttal of Peggy's (and Andre's) pretensions, challenging her cerebral obsession with art and consequent aloofness from Hollywood fandom, as well as from the studio whose career advice she has rejected.[10] In addition, the film pointedly recuperates melodrama as a genre, identifying Peggy's posturing as erroneous, by reuniting Peggy and Billy as co-stars on the set of a King Vidor World War I melodrama that references Vidor's *The Big Parade* (1925). With the director's warning to Billy as he steps into stardom—"don't let it enlarge your hatband"—and Peggy's discarding of her Patricia Pepoire persona, the film within the film becomes a confirmation of both stars' ability to represent model stars.

Fig. 1.3: *Show People* (MGM, 1928) uses comedy to return the pretentious "Patricia Pepoire" to the more acceptable identity of Peggy Pepper (played by Marion Davies).

In interviews promoting the film, Marion Davies pointed specifically to the breakdown of the star-audience relationship, drawing parallels between narrative events and her own experience of stardom. In the midst of Peggy's inflated egotism, the head of High Arts Studio reveals that her box-office appeal has dwindled to the extent that exhibitors are canceling her films. He attributes this solely to her excessive star persona: "You're not on the level with the public that made you—and from now on I want to see the *real* Peggy Pepper on the screen." An interview published in *Picture Play* in March 1928 suggests that Davies experienced her own period of adjustment to stardom, citing as an example her irritability at a costume issue on the set of *The Fair Co-Ed* (Sam Wood, 1927).[11] Audience response is again emphasized as the key factor in the reported shift in the star's behavior and self-imaging: "I shouldn't have been starred at first. The glamour of it appealed. From a simple home I went into the 'Follies.' With movie stardom, my every whim was satisfied. I believed, actually, that all I had to do was to walk across the screen in lovely settings, and let the public get an eyeful. They got it, stopped looking, and started criticizing."[12] The author, Myrtle Gebhart, informs readers that, consequently, "Marion is one of the few publicity-made stars who have buckled down to earnest work once they realized their insecure footing."[13] Davies even suggests she has collated fan critiques of her acting to consult as she focuses on her craft rather than stardom, as Gebhart notably comments, "With comedy she found herself."[14] The glamour of stardom is far from rejected, however, with full disclosure of Davies's extreme wealth, lavish homes, and legendary parties (pointedly without mention of her relationship with William Randolph Hearst),[15] although Gebhart fails to divulge that the string ensemble demanded by Patricia Pepoire was apparently Davies's own.[16]

The specter of forfeiting stardom exists in each of these films and connects them to the rise-and-fall narrative. The bridge forms most explicitly in *Show Girl in Hollywood* (Mervyn LeRoy, 1930), a semi-sequel to the Broadway narrative of *Show Girl* (Alfred Santell, 1928). *Variety*'s review recognized that the stardom narrative was already being established as a cycle or genre of films, while dismissing this example as "strictly routine . . . pushed through with the perfunctory attitude so typical of programmers of a 'star' series."[17] Yet the film displays some of the decade's hard-hitting realism with which its studio, Warner Bros., would become associated in both the gangster genre and the musical's combination of escapism and social critique. LeRoy would, indeed, go on to direct both *Little Caesar* (1931) and *Gold Diggers of 1933* (1933). Like its silent predecessor, the film stars Alice White (according to *Variety*, "First National's answer to Clara Bow")[18] as Dixie Dugan, who moves from stage understudy to movie star when she flees the economic woes of Broadway for Hollywood. Dixie represents another proactive movie-struck girl, grabbing an opportunity to perform "I've Got My Eye on You" from the failed show *Rainbow Girl* when she and the show's director Jimmy Doyle (Jack Mulhall) chance upon Hollywood writer-director Frank Buelow in a nightclub. Ignoring intimations of Buelow's casting couch tendencies, as well as Jimmy's romantic declarations, Dixie departs, proclaiming, "I'll be speaking to you and all the rest of the world over the Vitaphone." The narrative's exposure of Buelow as a fraud and philanderer parallels the lessons Dixie is required to learn about both stardom and the possibility of professional decline.

Analyses of the film by Chris Yogerst and Nicholas Emme have described it, respectively, as a "lighthearted satire"[19] with a narrative in which "moments of camp are plenty."[20] Promotional adverts were similarly ambivalent, promising "camera winks" and "saucy slaps," as well as a "Double Exposure of Hollywood!"[21] The latter element is suggested in part by the realist moments throughout the film that depict Hollywood filmmaking on the Warner Bros. First National lot (the film's pressbook even suggested that studio workers were encouraged to wander into shots[22]). Most notably, the film uses Dixie's second performance of "I've Got My Eye on You" being filmed on the sound stage to suggest an exposure of the sound film's new techniques, depicting not only the cameramen on set, but also lighting, microphones, an orchestra, and a Vitaphone technician.[23] The various angles from which we view the number demonstrate the magnitude of the production, as do the multitude of crew and studio personnel in attendance. At the same time, shots from a cameraman's viewpoint, as well as overhead shots, merge the real world and the fantasy in this number, as the spectacle of Dixie, a plethora of showgirls and showboys, and a giant mechanical face suggest both the demystification of the new musical genre's production process and an audience's closeup on an actress poised for stardom.

Moreover, the framing of the narrative in relation to fading movie star Donny Harris, the rejected wife of Buelow who befriends Dixie, lends the narrative a deeply melodramatic tone. With her career apparently over at age thirty-two, Donny confronts the "big lie" of Hollywood mythology when revealing to Dixie the empty rooms of her Hollywood mansion, which she retains only for her image, and singing "There's a Tear for Every Smile in Hollywood" (figure 1.4). Donny's portrayal by silent movie star Blanche Sweet, for whom 1930 would represent her final year of Hollywood filmmaking, apart from a brief appearance in Danny Kaye's *The Five Pennies* (Melville Shavelson, 1959), reinforces the pathos of this scene. Dixie's later egotistical behavior encouraged by Buelow therefore occurs in the context of the studios' treatment of female stars and the prevalence of professional decline. Donny again becomes the frame through which Dixie's lesson is learned and her reformation takes place. When Dixie lands the starring role in the film version of *Rainbow Girl* alongside a part for Donny, and the production is shut down due to Dixie's demands for her own rewrites, Donny's suicide attempt at the thought of a return to professional ruin is what brings about Dixie's recognition of the Hollywood community the narrative has promoted. As Dixie and the film's screenwriter, Jimmy, are reunited, Donny experiences a career revival, and the cast attends the successful premiere of *Rainbow Girl* alongside Loretta Young, Al Jolson, and Ruby Keeler, the film suggests that Dixie's redemption as the ideal

Fig. 1.4: *Show Girl in Hollywood* (Warner Bros., 1930). Fading movie star Donny Harris (played by Blanche Sweet) schools newcomer Dixie Dugan (played by Alice White) on the temporary nature of fame for women in Hollywood.

studio star is what heralds the success of this and every movie star. Observing Dixie watching herself on the screen in the remarkably spectacular number "Hang onto a Rainbow" serves to reinforce the ordinary and extraordinary nature of such stardom.

Rising and Falling

The possibility that stardom might slip away is an inherent theme of the above films, whether instigated by a star's desire for escape or brought about by disruption to the star-studio-audience relationship. *Modern Screen* was also still cautioning young women in 1932 that their desire for stardom could end in poverty, crime, and death by gas oven in a tiny flat, or that waitressing and a pistol shot to the head might be the conclusion to a declining career.[24] The films whose narratives most explicitly center on the ephemeral nature of stardom while simultaneously confirming its constancy in the case of the model star are the best known of the genre, not least due to repeated remakes. Warner Bros.' 2018 release of *A Star Is Born*—starring and directed by Bradley Cooper and co-starring Lady Gaga—is the fourth version of the film, and the second following the 1976 film starring Barbra Streisand and Kris Kristofferson (Frank Pierson) to be constructed around music rather than movie stardom. Both the 1937 drama and the 1954 musical—the latter is discussed in the next chapter—narrate tales of finding and losing Hollywood stardom and success, and are closely related to George Cukor's 1932 drama *What Price Hollywood?* Each of these five films depicts its rise-and-fall narrative through the rise of a female character and the fall of a male, establishing broad character types for the genre's contrasting cycle of films focusing on the decline of the older female star. Unlike the latter, wherein the validity of the system sometimes fails to be restored by the closing reel, the Hollywood versions of the rise-and-fall narrative spotlight the manufacture of stardom while simultaneously and consistently authenticating its myths.

A Star Is Born has been read as close to a remake of *What Price Hollywood?*, a conclusion aided by the origins and background of the films as David O. Selznick productions, and the fact of a number of scenes in *A Star Is Born* and its later iterations closely resembling those that appear in the earlier film. J. E. Smyth frames these films as the apotheosis of Selznick's agenda to represent Hollywood history on the screen. Selznick's attempt to record a history that bore some semblance to reality, she argues, "was a courageous attempt to face Hollywood's failures, forgotten names, and the industry's almost historical compulsion to make obsolete relics out of its living film-makers."[25] Strategies to provide historical accuracy included the implicit and explicit referencing of star biographies, as well as the use of the actual shooting script as a visual frame for the *A Star Is Born* narrative.[26]

With narratives consumed by the theme of stardom, however, these films are necessarily concerned with articulating mythology more than with documenting film history, albeit drawing on reported industry facts and rumors. *What Price Hollywood?* was adapted from an Adela Rogers St. Johns magazine story entitled "The Truth About Hollywood," which the author suggested was modeled on actress Colleen Moore and her alcoholic producer husband John McCormick.[27] Like *Bombshell*, *Show Girl in Hollywood*, and *A Star Is Born*, the film carries the ghost of Clara Bow, this trend indicating how the actress had become something of a symbol within the industry for the vagaries of stardom in Hollywood and its unpalatable afterlife. Selznick initially intended to star Bow in a film closely tied to her real-life story but eventually rejected the idea for reasons that range from Bow's declining appeal for audiences to weight issues.[28] The script was therefore transformed into a tale of stardom inspired by nuggets from various star biographies, including Hollywood scandals, society marriages and divorces, and press intrusion. However, for aspiring movie star Mary Evans (played by Constance Bennett), such realities are not intended to serve as the kind of warnings directed at the movie-struck girls, nor is the slow decline of the director who discovers her, Max Carey, played by Lowell Sherman, presented as a condemnation of the industry. The film's insistent mythologizing of stardom, and consequently of the studio system that creates it, remains the film's core focus.

The film's opening scene is essential to an understanding of the ways in which Mary embodies its concept of stardom and its relationship to fandom. Mary's consumption of the magazine's movie-star stories and the fashions and makeup they sell through star promotions speaks to the clearly defined strategies of the star system. As the scene cuts from advertisements to Mary applying lipstick and putting on stockings while she gauges her likeness to the originals, and she assumes the role of Greta Garbo opposite Clark Gable in *Susan Lenox* (Robert Z. Leonard, 1931) alongside a publicity shot (figure 1.5), the film articulates the practices of copying and the processes of identification through which fans were encouraged to engage with stardom.[29] The film visually suggests a blurring of the lines between fandom and stardom as Mary uses her bedroom mirror as a camera and the music from her phonograph as the soundtrack to her performance. When she pushes her bed back into the wall of her tiny apartment on her way to her waitressing job, the film additionally lays the foundation for Mary's star identity as "America's pal," referencing "America's sweetheart" Mary Pickford.

The scene that follows at the famous Brown Derby restaurant confirms Mary's ambition is to achieve stardom for herself, transforming her imitation of Garbo retrospectively into a rehearsal of her own imagined screen appearances. David Thomson suggests, "The brilliance of *What Price Hollywood?* is in seeing the chanciness of elevation, the way any pretty face could be the one given the right circumstances."[30] The narrative, however,

Fig. 1.5: *What Price Hollywood?* (RKO Pathé, 1932). Mary Evans (played by Constance Bennett) begins the journey from fan to star by imagining herself in Greta Garbo's place.

indicates something other than "chanciness." Mary has positioned herself in an arena where, as the film explicitly shows, industry insiders mingle, deals are done, and careers are made. The Brown Derby had opened in February 1929 and debuted the practice of having telephones at the tables for the use of the stars, producers and gossip columnists such as Hedda Hopper and Louella Parsons.[31] Mary's knowingness in this Hollywood business environment is evident as she snubs a screenwriter who offers to get her into pictures and makes fun of the "ham" hyperbole of the actor trying to sell his box-office appeal over the phone. Throughout the film, a variety of characters illustrate the potency of the stardom myth, from the flower seller outside the Brown Derby, who suggests to Max "I'd be another Marie Dressler," to Mary's maid Bonita (played by Louise Beavers), who later attempts to convince Max of her "motion picture ability" by singing a verse of "All of Me." Mary's drive, however, makes her approach to Max not a random but another purposeful act when she convinces another waitress to let her wait on him because "I'm looking for a break, and I'm gonna get it." Consequently, when the drunken Max takes her to his film premiere and she gets her name in *Hollywood Mirror*, and Max follows this with a bit part in his movie, the film suggests that Mary is less Max's discovery than her own.

Mary is required to learn, however, that ambition is insufficient when her performance proves unimpressive and we view her repeatedly rehearsing the role in her apartment. Again, this film makes clear that the movie screen is the site where star quality is revealed. After Max and studio head Julius Saxe (played by Gregory Ratoff) watch her test reel in the screening room while Mary observes from the projection booth, the narrative suggests that the award of a seven-year contract is the result of her determined ambition, readiness to work, and essential screen charisma. Disruption to the stardom Mary subsequently achieves occurs through a breakdown in the relationship between star and audience, developing the narrative theme of *Show People* further. Some of this critique is displaced onto her polo playing aristocrat husband Lonny Borden (played by Neil Hamilton), who attempts to school Mary in refined clothes and home décor and refers to Hollywood folk as "cheap and vulgar without knowing it." Like Lola in *Bombshell*, Mary comes to the defense of the filmmaking community, describing them as "kind and human, and not so doggone superior," and Lonny is rejected by Hollywood through a fan magazine article in which the two are photographed separately and his name is misspelt. Yet when the incompatible couple ultimately divorce and Mary's sophisticated lifestyle and privacy demands for her young son lead the press to question "Is 'America's Pal' Becoming High Hat?," it points to her need to maintain both her specific star image and the essential connection with her audience.

Still, however, the film demonstrates some ambivalence about the star-audience relationship. When Mary and Lonny are married and leave the church in a scene replicated as the funeral scene in the *A Star Is Born* films, the avarice of the crowds as they swarm around Mary until the veil is pulled from her head presents this relationship as one in which the star is wholly dehumanized. The setting for this critique at a church positions stardom as America's twentieth-century religion, usurping traditional myths with its gods and goddesses and sending its congregation of fans into moral bankruptcy. The media circus of the wedding produced for the newsreel cameras by Saxe Productions as a box-office booster highlights the studios' essential complicity in this battle for America's soul.

Similarly, Max's alcoholic decline and eventual suicide when he shoots himself in a melancholic haze are partly founded in his industry experience, as Max's persistent cynicism suggests. From his response to Mary's enthusiasm at receiving a seven-year contract—"Well, don't blame me"—to his quip on a signed photo in Mary's home—"I made you what you are today—I hope you're satisfied," and his admission to her "I'm dead inside" moments before he commits suicide, Max's decline appears to be attributed less conclusively to individual frailty than is the case in the characterization of Norman Maine in either of the Hollywood *A Star Is Born* narratives, serving to counter the paternalism of the studio head evident in all three films. The montage of images reconstructing Max's story that precedes his actions additionally mirrors the film's opening montage as Mary imagines her own stardom in parallel with existing star images, acting as a direct visual disruption of the mythology that dominates her narrative path. Similarly, throughout the film, text inserts of fan magazine and newspaper articles intervene in the star myth created by Mary's ambition, hard work, and charisma, and articulate a pervasive threat of scandal that might disturb the audience–star relationship.

The restoration of the myths of stardom and Hollywood is ultimately the film's aim, however, and is achieved through Mary's acceptance that, as Saxe reminds her, "You are a motion picture star. You belong to the public. They make you and they break you." The threat of scandal from press accusations of an illicit relationship with Max is therefore resolved, not by escaping to the south of France, but by studio-controlled publicity, a reunion with her reformed ex-husband, and a movie role as a sacrificing wife. Mary's star identity as "America's pal," the film suggests, is dependent on the legitimate demands of her fans, rather than the business priorities of Hollywood or the press.

Developing from the cautionary tale gifted by an experienced female star to a young newcomer in *Show Girl in Hollywood*, and the parallel rise and fall of a movie star and director disconnected by professions and a paternal relationship, the 1937 version of *A Star Is Born* cements the rise-and-fall narrative in the contrasting paths to and from stardom of a romantic couple. A script entitled "It Happened in Hollywood" was first brought to Selznick by William Wellman and Robert Carson, with various versions then worked on by writers including Ring Lardner Jr., Budd Schulberg, and Dorothy Parker.[32] When Wellman was officially awarded the "Best Writing, Original Story" Academy Award for *A Star Is Born*, he subsequently passed it to Selznick, pointing to Selznick's commanding input into the script. While Smyth asserts that the film was Selznick's attempt to make Hollywood "come to terms with its past, its willingness to forget or glamorize the uglier part of its history,"[33] Thomson, in contrast, suggests that Selznick's notes for the script's rewrite indicate that "he was fighting the inherent sourness of a director [Wellman] and a writer [Carson] toward Hollywood. He needed to think well of his world and what he did."[34] The script therefore shifted to minimize direct connections between the rise of Esther Blodgett/Vicki Lester (played by Janet Gaynor) and the fall of Norman Maine (Fredric March) and promoted a sense of destiny in Esther's stardom.[35]

The film is additionally less reliant on scenes of filmmaking than its antecedents or earlier examples of the stardom genre in constructing a realist sensibility. Like *What Price Hollywood?*, it draws on the histories of Hollywood stars including John Barrymore, John Gilbert, and John Bowers, as well as producer and first husband of Colleen Moore, John McCormick.[36] According to Axel Madsen, Selznick, in fact, thought Wellman's first draft was too derivative of Frank Fay and Barbara Stanwyck's marriage—Stanwyck having confided in Wellman about marriage difficulties during the filming of *The Purchase Price* (1932)—and ordered rewrites under legal advice.[37] In addition, the scene in which studio boss Oliver Niles (played by Adolphe Menjou) visits Norman Maine in a sanatorium is drawn from a tale related by George Cukor to Selznick of a similar visit he made to Barrymore in an effort to persuade him to take on the role of De Varville in *Camille* (1936).[38]

The use of the original final script as a framing device establishes a visual setting for the narrative of Hollywood documentation, which, at the same time, points to its fictional basis, a blurring of the lines between the real and the fictional similarly at play around the film's female star. The film's more significant framing device, however, and the one that establishes the mythical foundation of the film, occurs around Esther's grandmother Lettie (played by May Robson). The narrative opens with Esther and her younger brother returning home in the snow to the Blodgett family's "isolated farmhouse" after visiting the cinema to see a Norman Maine picture. Esther's Aunt Mattie (played by Clara Blandick) launches into an attack on Esther's obsession with the movies, fan magazines, and going to Hollywood. She cites as examples of her niece's inappropriate behavior Esther talking with a Swedish accent to a horse and practicing acting in a mirror, suggesting parallels with Mary Evans. Esther's resistance to marriage and defiant assertion of her right to self-determination becomes a declaration of independence: "What's wrong with wanting to get out and make something of myself . . . I'm going out and have a real life. I'm going to be somebody."

The narrative sets this rebellion explicitly in the context of the mythology of the West through Esther's grandmother, who relates Esther's desire for stardom to her own journey westward as a pioneer. In a transformation of patriarchal history into a modern myth of female aspiration, Lettie advises Esther that acting on her dreams is her "right," firmly tying the pursuit of Hollywood stardom to pioneer mythology with the affirmation, "There'll always be a wilderness to conquer; maybe Hollywood's your wilderness now" (figure 1.6). As Lettie secretly finances her granddaughter's journey to Hollywood and takes her to the train that she calls Esther's "prairie schooner," the film firmly establishes its narrative as a cross-generational her-story of American individualism.

The intertitle that follows introducing Esther's arrival in Hollywood—"HOLLYWOOD . . . the beckoning El Dorado . . . The Metropolis of Make Believe in the California hills . . ."—combines America's myth of the West with El Dorado's myth of its elusive prize. Esther's first stop at Grauman's Chinese Theatre, where she gazes at the foot- and handprints of such stars as Jean Harlow, Harold Lloyd, and Shirley Temple, relocates the narrative both geographically and mythically in Hollywood and the mythologizing of stardom at this iconic site. When she places her feet in the footprints of Norman Maine, the film sets up their dual narrative and explicitly points to Esther's usurping of Norman's stardom. After initial struggles that serve as the genre's conventional warning of the rarity of success, Esther is "discovered," like Mary Evans, through a combination of her ambition and active exploitation of an opportunity. Befriended by assistant director Danny McGuire (played by Andy Devine), who gets her a waitressing gig at a Hollywood party, she at first attempts to gain the attention of various influential partygoers with her impersonations of Garbo, Katharine Hepburn, and Mae West. When she catches the eye of an inebriated Norman Maine, whom she has so far observed from afar on the screen and in a drunken

Fig. 1.6: *A Star Is Born* (Selznick International Pictures, 1937). Grandmother Lettie (played by May Robson) encourages Esther (Janet Gaynor) in her quest for stardom as a modern parallel of her own pioneer experience.

fight with a photographer at the Hollywood Bowl, this occurs initially as a romantic attraction. Their subsequent relationship alongside Esther's ambition leads to both Norman's arrangement of her screen test for his film "The Enchanted Hour," and the essential alignment of Esther's rise with Norman's fall as a star, distinguishing the *A Star Is Born* series from, in particular, *What Price Hollywood?*

The film also takes the opportunity at this stage to both position Esther's forthcoming stardom in Hollywood history and to establish her success in fandom. While Norman assures Esther that "Harlow, Lombard, Myrna Loy" have each experienced similar nerves at their first screen test, the narrative displays Esther's performance neither on the set nor as viewed by studio head Oliver Niles. Instead, evidence of Esther's star quality is provided by the premiere of her first film as Vicki Lester, when we first see her on the screen, and by the rapturous response of movie fans, who immediately endorse their new star. Esther/Vicki's stardom therefore becomes the inevitable result of the processes of fandom and ambition to which the film has bound her characterization from the opening scenes.

Reviews and articles published around the time of *A Star Is Born*'s release continuously drew parallels between Esther Blodgett and Janet Gaynor through these tropes and that of stardom gained or regained. Gaynor's early period of stardom in silent cinema from *Seventh Heaven* in 1927 through to the first ever Academy Award for "Best Actress in a Leading Role" in 1929 had made her one of the period's top box-office stars, but her career had fragmented in the transition to talking pictures. In their reviews of *A Star Is Born*, for which she was nominated for another Oscar, *Life* magazine and *Screenland* both referred to Gaynor as "a star reborn,"[39] drawing attention to the career decline that they predicted would be reversed by her performance in Selznick's film. Both similarly depicted Gaynor's stardom narrative as one built on her own initial fandom, with *Life* suggesting that on leaving high school she "dreamed of being a star" and *Screenland* describing how as "a wistful big-eyed mite she gallantly stormed those same Hollywood gates."[40]

Other articles credited Selznick with the rebirth of Gaynor's stardom; *Silver Screen*, for example, suggested the producer had "snatched Janet Gaynor from comparative obscurity to dazzling new fame with a suddenness more striking than that of the story chosen for her triumphant rise on the screen."[41] Muriel Babcock in *Modern Screen*, however, refuted the idea that Gaynor's comeback was the result of the intervention of Selznick and Wellman, color photography, or having March as her leading man. Babcock instead depicted Gaynor as a savvy "Career Girl," wading through a macho culture at Fox and negotiating loan-outs "through skillful manoeuvering" so that, when presented with the opportunity of working on *A Star Is Born* with Selznick, "she found what she had been looking for, and she took it." Ultimately, Babcock suggested, "'A Star is Born' is only another milestone along the pathway she marked out for herself some years back. She deserves lots of credit."[42] The parallels drawn between star and character ambitiously translating movie fandom into movie stardom and, in Gaynor's case, the addition of a resurrected career, reemphasize the essential connections between star and audience made by both film and genre as a requirement for successful stardom.

The film additionally makes clear that Norman's faltering career is occurring through a combination of personal faults, audience disinterest, and corporate realities that make him an uninsurable box-office has-been. While his fall takes place alongside Esther's rise, the narrative avoids any suggestion of cause and effect, particularly through the establishment of these elements prior to her stardom. The dramatization of their oppositional paths remains central to the narrative though, made explicit in moments such as Vicki's name replacing Norman's on the poster for "The Enchanted Hour," just as he will subsequently be replaced by a younger male star in her next film; or Esther's embodiment of stardom as Vicki Lester accepting the Academy Award set in direct contrast with Norman's drunken stage invasion, when he inadvertently slaps Esther and requests awards for "the three worst performances of the year because I've earned them."

Norman remains fully invested in the myth of stardom, however, demonstrating this through his promotion of Esther and the key role he plays in articulating the film's mythology. As they look out over the city after the successful preview of "The Enchanted Hour" and Norman utters the words "a star is born," he points to the lights of Los Angeles as "a carpet spread for you," indicating the opportunities for success at Esther's feet provided by this Western land of opportunity. In this moment, the notion of stardom becomes fully mythologized around Esther in its mythical location. Norman's later suicide to prevent a scenario in which "there'll be no more Vicki Lester" only reinforces his key role in communicating the stardom myth.

In one of a number of scenes repeated from *What Price Hollywood?*—some of which would reoccur in additional remakes—the film again provides a limited space in which disruption to such mythology might occur. The church scene on this occasion follows Norman's funeral rather than the couple's wedding, suggesting the importance of Norman's demise as a function of Vicki's survival. The fans' dehumanization of stars, while wholly consumed by stardom's mythology, is therefore even more bleak, as the film depicts fans grasping for Vicki's attention until her black veil is torn from her head. By ultimately returning to its framing of female stardom in the mythology of the West, however, the film reasserts its promotion of the stardom myth.

With Esther on the point of departing Hollywood for the safety of small-town America, her grandmother's arrival in Hollywood serves as a reminder of the narrative's core conceit. Repeating her own pioneer journey West and tying it to Esther's Hollywood journey, Lettie reminds her granddaughter of the sacrifices demanded by ambition and success and restores her to the stardom she was on the point of rejecting. The two women become combined emblems of Western mythology—historic and modern—constructed around the pioneer settlers and Hollywood stardom. When Esther returns with her grandmother to Grauman's Chinese Theatre for her film's premiere and Lettie takes to the radio airwaves to encourage fans in their dreams of stardom—citing herself as an example of realized dreams—the film's framing of stardom in America's myth of the West becomes indisputable. By introducing herself to radio fans as "Mrs Norman Maine," Esther simultaneously recuperates Norman within this familial embodiment of stardom.

A Star Is Born represents Hollywood's essential star narrative, depicting stardom as a modern-day myth realizable through ambition, sacrifice, and fandom, and articulated by an actress whom the industry could similarly project as the embodiment of her movie-star character. The disruptions to such mythology that occur are ultimately resolved by the potency of the stardom myth and its foundation in Hollywood and American mythology. The 1954 narrative moves away from the classical drama of its predecessor to a combination of melodrama and musical that disturbs the thematic tone and representation of its 1930s sister, just as its postwar context and the star text of Judy Garland cause clear shifts in the narrative's depiction of the stardom myth. Several decades later, the critical attention Damien Chazelle's 2016 film La La Land received on its release largely revolved around its strong association with generic traditions, with a lack of reticence toward the integrated musical number unusual for a modern musical, and explicit referencing of the numbers and performers of earlier Hollywood and French musicals. The film's narrative, however, clearly positions La La Land as a stardom film on whose traditions it equally draws in its updating of the musical, demonstrating the persistence of the stardom film's form as well as its genre hybridity. La La Land's opening number, "Another Day of Sun," indeed operates as an ode to Hollywood stardom, while "Someone in the Crowd," "City of Stars," and "Audition (The Fools Who Dream)" each relates to the theme of Hollywood aspiration.

The film's core narrative conceit centers on the career ambitions of the two protagonists: actress Mia (played by Emma Stone), who works as a barista while auditioning in the hope of achieving movie stardom; and pianist Seb (played by Ryan Gosling), who dreams of opening a jazz club and maintaining the music's history. In a key early scene for the development of their romance and Mia's characterization, they stroll around the Warner Bros. lot where Mia works, passing sets where filming is taking place and peering into a soundstage. The scene refers to similar moments in various stardom films—in particular, *Singin' in the Rain*—as well as screenwriters Joe Gillis and Betty Schaefer's late-night stroll around the "drowsing" streets of the Paramount lot in *Sunset Boulevard* (Billy Wilder, 1950), as they take a break from their script while crews work on the sets.

At the same time, the scene provides an appropriately mythical setting in which to draw on the 1937 version of *A Star Is Born* as Mia explains to Seb her desire to act that springs from an affinity with Hollywood. Like Betty, who says of one of the sets "[all] cardboard, all hollow, all phony, all done with mirrors. You know, I like it better than any street in the world," Mia continuously expresses her love for the fictionalized reality before them, pointing like a fan to the window from which Ilsa and Rick looked out onto the streets of Paris in *Casablanca* (Michael Curtiz, 1942). Unlike Betty, however, Mia plans to translate her love for this mythical imagery into stardom. The aunt who acted with a traveling theatre company (an idea with its own air of mythical narrative) and introduced her to classic movies acts as a modern-day version of Esther Blodgett's grandmother, propelling Mia toward an ambitious crack at movie stardom. Lettie's warning to Esther that stardom demands sacrifice, in turn, comes to fruition in the relationship rupture which occurs when Mia's "break" in a starring role takes her to Paris. With a narrative conclusion that sees Seb open a successful jazz club and Mia as a fully fledged movie star, wife, and mother married to another man, the film departs from the narrative resolution that defines the majority of, if not all, musicals, while reinforcing its ties to *A Star Is Born*. The film's alternate ending reemphasizes the perfect myth of stardom as a fictional fantasy, constructing Mia, Seb, and offspring as a successful dual career family to the accompaniment of the "City of Stars" theme and visual references to classical musicals. The cinematic quoting of *Singin' in the Rain*'s "Broadway Melody" and Garland's tonally darker "Born in a Trunk" from *A Star Is Born* simultaneously point to *La La Land*'s overall ambivalence, with its veneration of the musical's fantasy core not wholly overwhelmed by its more realistic modern-day conclusion.

The combination of endings in *La La Land* pertinently stresses the film's roots in the stardom film and in a mythology that includes Lettie's universal truth of sacrifice. At the same time, its liberal referencing of other stardom films, not least of which are the generically different (but far from contrasting) versions of *A Star Is Born*, points to an enduring and essential genre hybridity. The next chapter explores the impact of genre on the representation of star mythology, considering the association of core narratives with musical, melodrama, and horror films, and the central significance of form and style in drawing out generic themes that intervene in the stardom narrative's established representation of star mythology.

2   GENRE AND HYBRIDITY

In Robert Aldrich's 1955 stardom narrative *The Big Knife*, Jack Palance plays the role of Hollywood star Charlie Castle desperately trying to extricate himself from the financial and creative control of studio head Stanley Hoff played by Rod Steiger. Based on Clifford Odets's stage play, the film opens with a credit sequence resembling a film noir cinematic version of Edvard Munch's *The Scream*, Palance grasping his head in torment. What follows is a searing critique of Hollywood's treatment of its actors, from the pimping of doomed starlet Dixie Evans (played by Shelley Winters) on the promise of stardom, to the threatening intrusiveness of the gossip columnist who enquires about Castle's sleeping arrangements with estranged wife Marion (played by Ida Lupino) while issuing veiled threats to expose his liberal politics or the scandal lurking in the corners of his successful career. Castle dreams of creative control under the artistic stewardship of directors like George Stevens, Joseph Mankiewicz, or Stanley Kramer, but his success has been built on swords-and-sandals epics and boxing movies in which Castle represents little more than a physical product displayed and beaten. Castle's stardom leaves him at the mercy of a studio head's manipulation, as Hoff blackmails him over a hit-and-run, and finally demands Castle cover up Hoff's own violent scandal using drugs and murder. Resisting another seven-year contract, the star's desperate drive for independence from a destructive, dividend-obsessed Hollywood is exposed as a futile endeavor by Castle's self-inflicted death in the final reel.

The mix of film noir and melodrama as a setting for this dark postwar tale seems wholly fitting for a narrative that aims to confront the kind of Hollywood mythology to which Castle has fallen victim. As the opening narration reveals: "Charlie Castle is a man who sold out his dreams, but he can't forget them." The myth of stardom, the film suggests, is what haunts him, and his inability to reconcile his dreams with the reality of the industry results in his emotional breakdown and the film's hard-hitting conclusion. Yet the stardom film's close association with the additional genres of the musical and horror means that narrative themes that are essential to films about stardom necessarily cross generic boundaries. Existing ties between these genres are found in notions of performance, excess, and gender, which similarly play out in the stardom film. As visual and thematic traits collide with stardom mythology as well as fluid genre hybridity, the range of representations that ensue provides for dramatizations of the star narrative that move beyond its broader archetypes.

Musical and Melodrama

Whether integrated through narrative and characterization or structured as distinct moments of spectacle, musical numbers assume an essential role in the musical genre that emphasizes and enhances the spectacle of stardom. In both the integrated and the aggregate form, musical performance occupies a space superseding that of the narrative and suspending its dominance, illustrated by star performers who, as Steven Cohan suggests, "can quite literally and quite spectacularly stop the show as proof of his or her extraordinary talent."[1] The genre lends itself with ease therefore to narratives in which characters' pursuit of stardom plays a central role, providing a dual emphasis on stardom through these narratives and the explicit embodiment of stardom by the star performers themselves. Simultaneously, musical performance becomes the means through which the genre expresses its own mythology, as Jane Feuer's key theory argues, celebrating a "myth of entertainment" as a representation of American democracy in a modern, egalitarian and inclusive (although not racially) form.[2] Paralleling the stardom film's central motif of stardom as the twentieth-century version of the pioneers' journey westward, the musical's mythology merges with that of the stardom narrative in an amplified promotion of the Hollywood agenda. Where musicals veer into less distinct genre territory, however, this hybridity opens a space in which the coexistence of these complementary myths is noticeably disturbed.

The famed 1952 musical *Singin' in the Rain*, directed by Gene Kelly and Stanley Donen, while most often considered in terms of its reflection on film history, also centers on the dual narrative strands of the maintenance and creation of stardom. Produced in the context of a declining Hollywood studio system and the rise of television, the film's narrative depicts the industry's earlier period of transition from silent cinema to sound, but does so by clearly outlining the kind of star who might successfully navigate through such change to a successful career. The film's opening at the premiere of the latest silent movie starring Don Lockwood (played by Kelly) and Lina Lamont (played by Jean Hagen), "The Royal Rascal," assumes strong audience awareness of the star system and its construction of fandom. The humorous depiction of a crowd of fans at Hollywood's Chinese Theatre being whipped into a frenzy of excitement by a gossip columnist as they await the arrival of the stars establishes the tone for the way we should receive the fictitious story of Don's path to stardom that he relates to listening fans. The clash of Don's voiceover narration, which suggests that playing symphony halls led to a barrage of calls from Hollywood, against the visual depiction of barrooms, burlesque, and a stretch as a movie stuntman, points to Don's complicity in a system that systemically deceives its audience. Indeed, the contrasting stories act as pre-parody of the road to stardom mythologizing that occurs in Kelly's "Broadway Melody" ballet.[3]

Each of the lead characters (other than Don's best friend and composer Cosmo, played by Donald O'Connor), in fact, presents a false impression of him/herself. Lina's persona as a sophisticated and humble star, for example, belies her demanding character and high-pitched voice, the latter hidden by the efforts of Don and studio head R. F. Simpson (played by Millard Mitchell) to silence her in public. When Don attempts to escape his adoring fans after the premiere and leaps from the top of a tram into Kathy Selden's (played by Debbie Reynolds) car—evoking the myth of stardom by seemingly dropping from the sky (figure 2.1)—the mockery of silent movie stars she expresses and her pretensions to a classical career on the Broadway stage will be exposed as a sham when she admits her moviegoing fandom and moves from the Coconut Grove floor show to the chorus of the movie musical.

Fig. 2.1: *Singin' in the Rain* (MGM, 1952). Escaping his adoring fans, movie god Don Lockwood (Gene Kelly) drops heaven-sent into a car driven by Kathy Selden (Debbie Reynolds).

The industry's shift from silent to sound means that only Lina is pun-ished for this culture of dishonesty, despite her childlike belief in the fake relationship with Don written about in the fan magazines. The adaptation of "The Duelling Cavalier" into the "All Singing. All Talking. All Dancing" musical "The Dancing Cavalier" underlines *Singin' in the Rain*'s generic promotion of the "myth of spontaneity,"[4] valuing those performers who are able to "burst into song" or dance and, in this case, speak in an appro-priate tone, pitch, and accent for the screen. Just as the melodrama has to be rescued from the tortured failure of its attempt to introduce sound by an apparently seamless production of a musical version, Lina's inability to transition from a silent movie star of the past to a musical star of Holly-wood's new era separates her from both her co-star and from Kathy, who closes the film on a poster starring opposite Don in Monumental Pictures' self-reflective musical "Singin' in the Rain" in a reinvigoration of the star-dom myth. As Gerald Mast suggests: "In a filmusical, only a whole per-former is a whole human being."[5] Lina's downfall is ultimately assured by her attempt to sabotage Kathy's career when she threatens to sue the studio unless Kathy is kept offscreen to dub her vocals and the studio ceases promoting her as their new musical star. When Don and Cosmo join forces with R. F. to expose Lina's inadequacy to the film audience by pulling up the stage curtain to reveal Kathy singing as Lina mimes, the act punishes her for both her lack of ability as a performer and her unsuitability as a studio star.

As Cohan points out, this containment of Lina's unruliness contrasts with the treatment of Don, who has his co-star dubbed without her approval and apparently produces a musical with minimal assistance or intervention from the head of the studio.[6] An early version of the screenplay in which the theatre scene presents Kathy struggling as Don covers her mouth suggests that her experience of stardom was not necessarily envisaged as one free of the kind of silencing that Lina experiences. A final scene that brings Kathy and Don to the Chinese Theatre as the married co-stars of "Broadway Rhythm," however, has Lina suffering an even worse fate, introduced by the columnist as Cosmo's new wife and "the former Lina Lamont. She is now appearing in 'The Jungle Princess,' in which she doesn't say a word—she just grunts!"[7]

George Cukor's 1954 remake of *A Star Is Born*, drawing also on his earlier film *What Price Hollywood?*, represents a tonal shift from its predecessors brought about through its genre hybridity—Warner Bros. termed the film "a comedy drama with musical interludes"[8]—and the prominent space Judy Garland occupies in the film's depiction of stardom. Much of the film's history has been bound up in a production background of battles between Warner Bros. and producers Garland and then-husband Sid Luft over the studio's extensive cuts and its subsequent 1983 restoration,[9] as well as Garland's unexpected Academy Award loss to Grace Kelly in *The Country Girl* (George Seaton, 1954), all of which lends this version its own mythological status and suggests an essential meta-narrative. The ways in which the film veers between musical and melodrama, however, along with its potent use of color, late script additions, and Garland's role in occupying both lead characterizations result in a film that represents one of the darkest and most conflicted of Hollywood's stardom tales.

Even as press reports suggested budget issues and production delays during filming,[10] Warner Bros.' marketing for *A Star Is Born* stressed both Garland's talent as a performer and the film's significance as her return to the screen after what the studio described as a hiatus following *Summer Stock* (Charles Walters, 1950). Ignoring MGM's firing of the star in 1950, production notes nevertheless alluded to a new and improved Garland after the experience of a critically acclaimed international tour of venues that included the London Palladium and New York's Palace Theatre. Warner Bros., suggesting echoes of both the press positioning of Janet Gaynor's performance as a comeback and of the studio's remodeling of Esther Blodgett in the film, promoted Garland as a movie star reborn, declaring: "The confidence, poise and experience Judy gained in this tour she brought to the screen for her role of Esther Blodgett, re-named Vicki Lester."[11]

Even more explicit connections were made between Garland and her character that tied both to a Hollywood history of female stardom. Just as Norman Maine makes these links in both films—in this version referencing the stage and film actress Ellen Terry—Warner Bros.' marketing drew attention to the scrapbook Esther shows to Norman (played in this version by James Mason) on the night they first meet and that she brings with her to the studio's publicity department on her arrival as a contract player. Suggesting this was "no ordinary prop. It once belonged to Colleen Moore and is filled with newspaper and magazine stories about her early career as a Warner Bros. star," a studio short feature story related that "Between scenes of 'A Star is Born,' Judy read with interest the articles about the screen beginning of Miss Moore, a top star in her day"[12] (figure 2.2). Such direct connections being made between Garland, Esther, and the star of *Ella Cinders* and inspiration for *What Price Hollywood?* reemphasizes the extent to which this version of *A Star Is Born* was bound up in the mythology of stardom constructed through its screen antecedents and the consistent influence of Garland's star identity.

The generic shift of the film enables the referencing of both Garland's screen career and its attendant imagery. Marketing reported that the star referred to aspects of the "Someone at Last" number as "Early Judy Garland,"[13] while the narrative of the "Born in a Trunk" number which plays out on screen at the theatre preview of Esther's first starring role references Garland through child performance and show business history, just as it signals through Garland's recognizable talent Esther's ability to become a movie star. More significantly, the difficulty of repeating the earlier film's depiction of Esther as an inexperienced hopeful due to the

Fig. 2.2: *A Star Is Born* (Warner Bros., 1954). Judy Garland's arrival as Esther Blodgett in the studio's publicity department carrying Colleen Moore's scrapbook positions each of the women in the history of Hollywood stardom.

casting of Garland means that a shift occurs in the narrative's characterization of Esther and her desire for stardom.

While the stardom achieved by Mary Evans and Gaynor's Esther Blodgett is the result of the ambition they immediately exhibit and act upon, and which is closely associated with their fandom, as a band singer with a developing career, Garland's Esther initially displays little ambition for movie stardom. In fact, when she suggests her dream is discovery by a record company scout leading to a number one record, Norman responds, "There's only one thing wrong with that . . . It might happen very easily. Only, the dream isn't big enough." Norman's use of Ellen Terry's description of star quality as "that little something extra" (interestingly, a very late script addition in February 1954),[14] and his identification of this in Esther, is what sparks her belief that the bigger dream of Hollywood stardom is achievable, and indicates his discovery of her as a potential star. She underlines this lack of inherent desire to become a movie star when she explains to piano player Danny McGuire (played by Tom Noonan): "He gave me a look at myself I've never had before. He saw something in me nobody else ever did. And he made me see it too. He made me believe it." The career of Esther's character in the "Born in a Trunk" number is depicted as one of ambition and hard work followed by discovery when the character is found singing "Melancholy Baby" in a supper club by a movie producer. Yet without the film's prior establishment of Esther's persistent desire or association with fandom, ambition is refracted consistently through Norman.

During the script's development, Cukor recognized this displacement, making a file note to discuss the issue with screenwriter Moss Hart:

> I think we have lost one element of the original picture. Janet Gaynor had a dream to go to Hollywood—that was working for us. In our case, Judy has a different dream, and it is Norman who tells her to go after bigger things. Somehow, I would like to indicate that after this she has an ideal and a dream. It will be more moving when she gives all this up.[15]

While the film depicts Esther's rise to stardom, this explicit expression of Esther's desire never fully occurs. As Norman facilitates opportunities, from arranging a screen test to getting her singing voice to the ears of studio head Oliver Niles (played by Charles Bickford), which results in a starring role, Esther's stardom is framed through his ambitions for her, lending her desire for movie stardom a lingering ambiguity, even as she works to maintain it through Norman's decline.

The film's depiction of its rise-and-fall narrative occurs through a darker lens than its predecessors, particularly as a direct remake of the 1937 version, due to both the bleaker depiction of Norman's story as portrayed by Mason and the parallels drawn with Garland's star identity. Cary Grant had, in fact, been the initial preference of Garland and Luft for the role of Norman Maine, the two producers lobbying him personally so that Grant went so far as to rehearse a few scenes privately with Cukor. According to the producers' daughter, Lorna Luft, Grant's reluctance to engage with the psychology of Norman's alcoholic decline combined with his wariness about the potential difficulties of working with Garland ultimately steered him away from the project.[16] Mason's screen image was, in any case, much better suited to the dark melodrama that the film becomes. From the violent sexual tension of British films like *The Man in Grey* (Leslie Arliss, 1943) with Gainsborough Studios to the essential fatalism of *Pandora and the Flying Dutchman* (Albert Lewin, 1951), Mason's screen image carried a sense of romantic tragedy that befits the intensely melodramatic tone of *A Star Is Born* and his characterization of a star in decline.

The film's opening "Night of Stars" benefit immediately sets up Esther and Norman as two contrasting performers, with Norman introduced as an uncontrollable star violently disrupting proceedings backstage and resisting the attempts of the studio's head of publicity Matt Libby ("Libby")—played by Jack Carson—to manage him. The "Gotta Have Me Go With You" number with the Glenn Williams Orchestra—presented not in Garland style but as the controlled performance of a band singer—establishes Esther as a supreme professional, thus marking her ability to be transformed into an effective studio star. Norman's stage invasion during the number therefore provides the opportunity not only for their meet cute, but for her to demonstrate her professionalism again by rescuing the number and saving Norman from himself, prefacing how she will attempt to do this throughout the narrative when she marries him, persuades him to enter a sanatorium, enlists Oliver to offer him an acting role, and liberates him from a judge's jail sentence.

The impact of Garland's compelling star image, however, means that while parallels might be drawn with Esther's rise to the heights of Hollywood stardom in the studio system, as Garland herself suggested, awareness of the star's reported issues of substance abuse, suicide attempts, and repeated production difficulties at MGM—this film was, indeed, being marketed as a comeback—means that Garland is additionally aligned with Norman's unruly stardom and periods of decline. Perhaps most potently, Esther's lament to Oliver about Norman's self-destructive behavior when he visits her on the set of the "Lose That Long Face" number draws Garland's well-publicized breakdowns and prescription drug issues into the narrative. As Esther describes watching Norman "crumble away bit by bit, day by day, in front of your eyes," the film's exploitation of Garland as a reference point for the characterization of Norman becomes clear (figure 2.3).

The use of color in the explicit representation and implicit referencing of stardom, as well as ambivalent attitudes toward the studio system, is a key aspect of the film, to which Warner Bros.' marketing drew substantial attention. The film's Special Color Design Adviser, photographer George Hoyningen-Huene, was featured prominently in marketing, arguing "Color pictures usually have too much color . . . It is used indiscriminately. There is no co-ordination and no dramatic relationship between color of costumes, sets, makeup and props." *A Star Is Born* had a purposeful strategy, he insisted, which meant "Instead of permitting just any color to get into a scene and react on the consciousness of the audience, we selected our colors carefully, so that each had something to do with the mood or

Fig. 2.3: *A Star Is Born* (Warner Bros., 1954) draws on Judy Garland's personal history for her experience of husband Norman Maine's self-destructive decline.

characterization."[17] Navy is a color associated with Esther throughout the narrative, for example, and the browns and oranges that dominate the sanatorium scene and suggest "bad taste and a depressing attempt at cheerfulness"[18] are introduced earlier in more palatable form in the couple's home when Norman learns from Oliver his fate is that of an ex-contract star, suggesting how Norman's decline will work to disturb his relationship with Esther. The film returns to these colors in the couple's home toward the film's conclusion when the threat emerges of Esther's self-destruction as Vicki Lester following Norman's suicide.

The moods created in these and additional scenes via strategic use of color mirror those of melodramas of the period and color noir musicals such as *Young at Heart* (Gordon Douglas, 1954) and *It's Always Fair Weather* (Stanley Donen and Gene Kelly, 1955), rather than color functioning as spectacle in archetypes of the musical genre. The impact on musical numbers amid this hybridity is best illustrated by "The Man That Got Away," the number through which Norman reveals to the audience Esther's essential star charisma. When the camera follows Norman into the empty Downbeat Club, we witness his reaction as he observes Esther singing after hours, something which is presented—in contrast to the "Night of Stars" number—as a naturalistic Garland performance as she interacts with the band and sings in an emotionally expressive style. The dimly lit, intimate scene additionally establishes Esther's ties to the mood of foreboding that circulates around Norman through the color palette of brown-toned furniture and orange-accented walls that accompany the navy of Esther's dress and the band's suits. Two alternative versions of the scene filmed earlier that included variants of larger crowds, bright lighting, pastel décor, and wardrobe shifts for Esther from pink and purple to brown, as well as alternative staging of Garland's whole performance,[19] reinforce the extent to which color and its alignment with mood, tone, character, and narrative became a focus of the final version of the scene and of the film overall.

The film's critique of the studio system similarly comes in narrative and visual form but exhibits the ambivalence of the stardom genre. The attempts of the male studio makeup technicians to transform Esther into their vision of a star by making her a confused combination of Dietrich and Crawford mirror a similar scene played with Janet Gaynor. This surgical version points to a harsher critique, however, the room's monochromatic grays suggesting, as Hoyningen-Huene described it, "the very scientific, the cold, clinical part of an actress' career."[20] The paternal figure that Oliver Niles represents in Esther's life and career, as well as his support of Norman as a star against both Libby and "the New York boys" who release him from his contract, means that critique is displaced away from the production arm of the studio and onto the untrustworthy business of publicity. Esther's first encounter with the studio as a contract player is in the publicity offices where the mantra "Glad to have you with us" repeated in gray-walled offices suggests an assembly line system, and the central role of the publicity machine in manufacturing stardom is emphasized when Esther has difficulty escaping the turnstile gate on her exit.

Despite this displacement developed further in the unsympathetic portrayal of Libby, who characterizes Hollywood's corporate detachment, the publicity scenes were, in fact, another late script addition,[21] suggesting that such a negative commentary on the star system was a less essential focus of the film than it might seem. The most severe depiction of the impact of the studio's business workings is associated with the audience, and is evident in a repeat of the church scene initiated in *What Price Hollywood?* at the wedding and moved to Norman's funeral in both versions of *A Star Is Born.* The cruelty of a fan lifting Esther's veil from her face in an attempt to fully view her despair—a moment with its origins in Norma Shearer's attendance at the 1936 funeral of her husband, MGM "Boy Wonder" Irving Thalberg[22]—nevertheless suggests the end result of the packaging of stars as products for consumption by a hungry audience. The "glittering white" glamour of the Academy Awards event, however, and the "blue green to express sad nostalgia" during Norman Maine's late-night visit to the Cocoanut Grove,[23] point to an ultimate postwar regret about a Hollywood lost to television, suburbia, and economic insecurity (even despite Norman's distasteful trawling for starlets). When the film comes full circle with Esther returning to the Shrine Auditorium to reclaim her stardom and restore Norman's status in Hollywood history, the film explicitly reasserts the validity of the stardom myth and implies its ability to endure.

Melodrama, Woman's Film, and Film Noir

Stardom films that fit more succinctly into the genre of melodrama and its intersections with the woman's film and film noir have often unsurprisingly found their emotional intensity in narratives centered on the loss of stardom. In contrast with escape narratives depicting the acquisition of stardom as freedom from control and restriction, and the rise-and-fall dual narrative, which has at its core the construction and reassertion of the stardom myth, films within this genre center on single-protagonist stories of stardom found and lost. With even the rise element, when included, serving only to frame the subsequent fall, the lack of compensating mythology offers little respite from the narratives' persistent sense of personal and professional tragedy. These films at the same time offer insights into cinematic and industry perspectives on male and female stardom as the narratives address career decline in contrasting ways.

While narratives focused on female stardom form the most extensive and best-known series of these films, those about male stars who experience success taken from their grasp represent an interesting diversion from the norm. Most notably, while narratives frequently connect their female protagonists' disappearing stardom to their physical appearance and therefore become critiques at varying levels of Hollywood's gendered attitudes to aging, the male star's decline is individualized as the result of either character traits or behavior deemed unacceptable, or the disruptive force of scandal. In *The Oscar* (Russell Rouse, 1966), the ambitious rise to stardom of Stephen Boyd's movie star, narrated in flashback by his friend—played by Tony Bennett—details the manipulation and abusive behavior that stimulates his decline. While he claws his way back to the Academy Award nomination that frames the narrative, his humiliating loss acts as Hollywood's rejection of an improper form of stardom. In *The Comic* (Carl Reiner, 1969), Dick Van Dyke's silent movie comic narrates his own story, illustrating the egoism that leads to his career's disappearance. As the narration is constantly contradicted by its visual depiction (a less benign use of contrast than in the case of Don Lockwood), the star is left a lonely figure yearning for a lost career.

Mirroring the combination of melodrama and thriller defining *Souls for Sale*, *Hollywood Boulevard* (Robert Florey, 1936) presents John Halliday's distinguished aging star as an actor written about in the newspapers only when his tailor is suing him for payment, and for whom even character parts are now out of reach. When John Wellington Blakeford is persuaded to reclaim his fame by selling his memoirs to a scandal magazine and the ghostwriter's scandalous take on Blakeford's love life revitalizes his film career but begins to damage his relationships, the actor's decision to reject notoriety aims to send an early Hollywood message that exploiting scandal is bad for business and for stardom. His reemergence as a star, however, suggests that a little relationship trouble and even a gunshot wound were worth the reward. Later, Hollywood attempts to defend both Hollywood stars and the movie industry against scandal magazines in the 1957 film *Slander* (Roy Rowland). The threat from the publisher (played by Steve Cochran) of a *Confidential*-style magazine to expose a male children's television entertainer's past (played by Van Johnson) as an armed robber unless he assists the magazine with a story on the drug-taking of a female movie star risks damaging two stars' careers through scandal. The TV star's refusal to succumb to intimidation results in temporary audience backlash and the consequential death of his young son, but the target of the film is its real loser when the publisher is shot dead by a mother appalled by her son's ethical deterioration and himself becomes the news story. Moreover, the film's implicit referencing of Ingrid Bergman's period as star pariah a few years earlier, when her extramarital relationship with Roberto Rossellini (whom she would later marry) saw her hounded out of Hollywood by religious groups, politicians, and the press, suggests more broadly an overriding theme that nothing good emerges from assaults on a movie star's image.

Films centering on male stories of stardom in decline, therefore, often allow their stars to reassume their star status at some level, or suggest their flagging career is the result of character flaws, individualizing the narratives and setting any industry critique in the context of star misbehavior. The familiar paths tread by female characters in this narrative strand, in contrast, overwhelmingly reveal how Hollywood becomes a hostile space for older female stars, as their appearances are deemed less appropriate to the construction of a feminine ideal. Narratives depict a male-dominated industry unsympathetic to women's attempts to reignite their stardom, often viewing such ambition as delusion, and expecting instead an acceptance of the inevitability of a career in the past, with humiliation and ultimate dismissal the result of resistance. The films seem to suggest that the characters prompted to go west in earlier narratives in pursuit of Hollywood's myth of stardom as female empowerment are themselves here discarded, just as older female characters at the edges of those films had warned. The dominance of female stars of the 1930s and 1940s in these films, however, adds a layer of critique that the films fail to extinguish. Drawing on star images constructed through earlier melodramas and the woman's film genre, whose narratives frequently centered on the confrontation of culturally defined gender norms, these stardom films become, rather, potent commentaries on Hollywood's gendered myth of stardom.

A key example of how these dichotomies play out is the 1952 Bette Davis film *The Star* (Stuart Heisler, 1952). The script was written by Katherine Albert and Dale Eunson, friends of Joan Crawford, with its origins in a novel published by Albert in 1939, and Albert's husband Eunson later confirmed the novel was based on Crawford's life.[24] Davis reaffirmed the film's basis in Crawford's story in a 1983 interview in *Playboy*, while simultaneously distancing the characterization from her own brand of stardom: "Oh, yes, that *was* Crawford. I wasn't imitating her, of course. It was just that whole approach of hers to the business as regards the importance of glamour and all of the offstage things."[25] For Davis, the film provided her ninth Academy Award nomination, but failed to increase the flow of lead roles that had been diminishing for several years. Even Davis's critically acclaimed performance in Joseph Mankiewicz's *All About Eve* (1950) and additional Oscar nomination had failed to reignite her film career, sending her to the stage in late 1952 with the musical revue *Two's Company*. While exhaustion and ill health eventually led to her early release from the Broadway production, it was not before *New York Times* theatre critic

Brooks Atkinson had concluded that "this episode in her career is likely to be a wounding one."[26]

The Star is one of several self-referential stardom films in which Davis dramatizes the dynamic in the relationship between stars and the stage and screen industries. Exploring Davis's performances in *Dangerous* (Alfred E. Green, 1935), *All About Eve*, *The Star*, and *What Ever Happened to Baby Jane?* (Robert Aldrich, 1962), Karen Beckman points to the agency inherent in Davis's repeated association with characters who resist being pushed from the spotlight. Her embodiment of the figure of the fading female star, Beckman argues, results in a star image that "refuses to vanish silently and instead emerges as a force that reshapes the vanishing woman's relationship with the medium that made her so visible in the first place."[27]

Davis's star image alongside her core status as a leading actress of the melodrama/woman's film genre of the 1930s and 1940s are immediately introduced as reference points in *The Star*'s opening scenes when her movie star character, Margaret Elliot, lingers outside an auction house. A searchlight and a publicity shot of a young Elliot/Davis are advertising an auction of Margaret's personal effects being held to pay off the star's debts, both the event and the photograph emphasizing her physical and financial decline (figure 2.4). As Christopher Ames describes, the film draws on the essential contrast between a youthful screen image and an aging reality inherent to cinema, as well as the screen's potential to create a visual narrative of aging, that we see through both Elliot and Davis here: "The ability to capture a moving human form on film was initially heralded as offering an immortality of sorts, but it also chronicles the ageing of a star across a career and offers repeated reminders of the difference between the ageing actor and the ageless image."[28] The auctioneer utilizes the mythology of stardom that created Margaret Elliot to make a sale, simultaneously positioning her stardom firmly in the past: "She *was* your favourite movie star. You stood in line to see her latest picture. She made you laugh; she made you cry; you were secretly in love with her. Show Margaret Elliot you haven't forgotten." Her agent's purchase of a crystal candelabra on the basis that "someone was going to buy it" commences the film's setting of Margaret's narrative in an industry in which male economic power and ideas of spent female stardom control her career.

Fig. 2.4: *The Star* (20th Century Fox, 1952). An auction promoting the sale of Margaret Elliot's (Bette Davis) personal belongings defines her youth and stardom in the past.

While the ex-husband she supported during their marriage now has a flourishing career in westerns, a luxury home, and a stay-at-home wife currently raising Margaret's young daughter Gretchen (played by Natalie Wood), Margaret's ambition to regain her success is presented, in contrast, as a foolish notion. Her agent Harry Stone (played by Warner Anderson) advises her candidly, "You're going to have to face a few facts . . . There's no denying that fresh, dewy quality, well, something else takes its place." He reinforces industry attitudes and therefore the inevitability of Margaret's career spiral downward with the revelation that rising young star Barbara Lawrence (playing herself) is now a client. Lawrence represents the direct replacement of experience with youth, having been signed by the producer of "The Fatal Winter," which Margaret had previously optioned as a novel and now views as her opportunity for a comeback. Margaret's persistent resistance, the film suggests, is futile and simultaneously against the natural order inherent to both the industry and her gender. While Margaret proclaims, "They can't put me out to pasture. Not me. I was a star," and a waitress excitedly recognizes her, the film's repeated message is that retirement and domestic bliss are her only sanctioned path. Moreover, *The Star* suggests that Margaret's stardom has always been a disruptive force. Margaret's economic provision has emasculated the brother-in-law who leaves a trail of failed businesses behind him and resulted in her own broken marriage blamed on Margaret's ambition and financial power. The film explicitly pitches two versions of womanhood against each other, as ex-husband John's second wife Faith (played by Fay Baker) relishes telling Margaret: "His name was Morgan. He didn't like being Mr. Elliot, living in Miss Elliot's house, entertaining Miss Elliot's guests. Why, he wasn't even Miss Elliot's husband. He was her lover, by appointment, when she wasn't too tired, or afraid to muss her hair." While Margaret accuses the couple of having conducted a clandestine affair and dismisses the "pure soap opera" style of her husband's second marriage, the narrative validates Faith's feminine identity as it continuously constructs Margaret's future as a choice between career frustration and familial contentment.

Of course, the choice is not fully Margaret's but principally Hollywood's, something the film fails to address, instead stressing the virtues of relinquishing stardom for the traditional roles of wife and mother. When Margaret is arrested after taking her Oscar on a drunken drive past the homes of young movie stars (calling out Mitzi Gaynor and Jeanne Crain for their youth adds a taste of realism), shipyard owner Jim Johanssen, played by Sterling Hayden, for whom Margaret had previously initiated a brief screen career, reverses these roles by rescuing her from a night in jail and eviction from her rented apartment. He continues to represent the security and traditional values that a life away from the screen would provide—emphasized by Hayden's physicality and deep voice—as he moves her into his home and promotes a down-to-earth lifestyle that contrasts with her star identity. Margaret's constant referencing of her movies as though they were examples of her own lived experience suggests that stardom has all but erased her identity and femininity, leaving her unable to engage with life beyond the screen.

Jim additionally critiques her sexuality, telling her, "I once thought you were a woman. I was wrong. You're nothing but a career." Margaret's theft of a bottle of perfume named "Desire Me" from a drugstore points to the need for adoration her stardom satisfies, as well as the relationships the narrative indicates her stardom has replaced. When the perfume turns out to be a display bottle full of water, Jim articulates its explicit symbolism: "When you grabbed it, you thought it was real. That's the story of your life, isn't it?" Jim assumes Margaret's position is the self-inflicted result of lavish spending, and has to be corrected by the star who explains she was once labeled "box-office poison," a reference to the title given to Joan Crawford by the National Theatre Distributors of America in 1938. Moreover, Margaret's challenge to the industry's narrative about her declining status mirrors elements of Davis's career as the character informs Jim that her refusal of poor roles meant she was forced to turn to independent production, suffering distribution issues caused by the larger companies, all leaving her with financial insecurity, even as the studio made millions from her films.

Margaret's submission to Jim's advice to live in the "real" world is temporary; she quits on her first day selling lingerie in a department store after hearing two older female customers discussing her arrest. Her declaration—"I *am* Margaret Elliot, and I intend to *stay* Margaret Elliot"—signals her intent to realize her own desires by retaining her stardom and rejecting the binary options of a vanishing Hollywood career or a traditional relationship (figure 2.5). When she presses her agent to get her a screen test for the lead role in "The Fatal Winter," the film's depiction of a paternalistic producer, not unlike Oliver Niles in *A Star Is Born*, suggests an industry taking care of its own rather than the repeated sabotaging of an Oscar-winning career. Joe Morrison (played by Minor Watson) thinks of stars as "so naughty, like children. At the same time, they're so appealing, also like children." By offering to test Margaret for the role of the older sister while casting rising star Barbara Lawrence as the eighteen-year-old lead, his actions are therefore presented as an uncommercial act of benevolence aimed at stemming an emotional breakdown.

In the face of such apparent compassion, Margaret, then, becomes the architect of her own downfall, as her unwillingness to be characterized as frumpy and middle-aged is presented as vain folly. Arguing with the director that "women of 42 these days don't have to look ready for the old people's home," she pointedly appropriates Lawrence's dressing room to remodel her character's appearance in a younger, more attractive vein, and the test performance that follows is presented as a master class in star

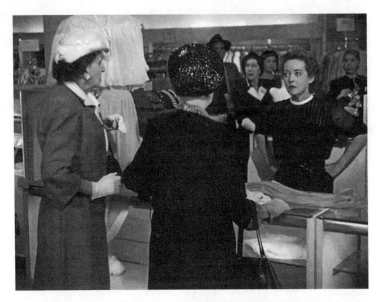

Fig. 2.5: *The Star* (20th Century Fox, 1952). "I *am* Margaret Elliot, and I intend to *stay* Margaret Elliot."

vanity. Her familiarity with the crew and references to working with cinematographer Ernest Laszlo, accompanied by Morrison's false assurance that the test is "just a formality" and her dismissal of scene direction, suggests star power at work. Davis, herself, admitted usurping her directors when she felt it necessary. However, the scene also references Crawford's constant use of "Bless you" to salute the crew.[29] When Margaret plays the scene with youthful flirtatiousness, it therefore suggests a deluded unwillingness to transition into an older screen identity.

At the same time, the scripted dialogue somewhat validates Margaret's take on the scene, as the male character opposite suggests, "You used to be quite a girl. You still think you are, don't you?" The young director's admiration for this New York stage actor and contrasting dismissal of Margaret's talents as those of a narcissistic movie star—"Fine, fine. Your fans would love it."—indicate an artistic snobbery that conflicts with Hollywood's aim to combine art with entertainment. Still, Margaret's punishment for failing to listen to male direction at every turn comes in her pain and humiliation when, watching the test alone, she realizes what she thought was an opportunity to restore her career has been lost. As a melodrama, the isolation of Margaret's outbursts of emotion at moments such as this when she despairs for her fragile grip on stardom reinforces a nontraditional emotional life centered on career rather than relationships.

The film's concluding scenes provide the sense of a warm and sympathetic industry sending Margaret off into the sunset of a family life, rather than the less favorable reality of a star succumbing to Hollywood's youth obsession and the limited choices it now offers her. Finding herself at a party at her agent's home where she has sought escape from her professional embarrassment, Hollywood insiders attempt unsuccessfully to reminisce with the star broken by her recent experience. Instead, she suffers the ignominy of watching the feted arrival of Barbara Lawrence following the successful preview of her latest film, as well as the news that another actress has been cast in the role of the older sister in "The Fatal Winter." When a young producer acknowledges her screen charisma, commenting "It's quite a face," and expresses his eagerness to cast her in a film being developed, her agent assures him that "Margaret has faced some facts today."

"Falling Star," the producer relates to Margaret, is a tale not of a dedicated actress but a determined movie star, "the ones that play it 24 hours a day . . . demanding, driving, ambitious." The producer, essentially articulating *The Star*'s message to Margaret, explains that the character will provoke not sympathy but "profound pity, worthy of the gods. This is a great tragedy. Why, my character is denied her birthright, the privilege and the glory of just being a woman." The film concludes by suggesting that this "Hollywood story" is written as a universal narrative about an ambitious woman who "can't face the fact that it's over," and offers a heavy-handed directive to its female audience as Margaret makes the choice to leave behind an opportunity to restore her star status, retrieves her daughter, and rushes to Jim in pursuit of an ideal of motherhood and marriage. *New York Times* critic Bosley Crowther's review of Davis's character as "repulsive," "pathetic," and "sad" in her unwillingness to accept what he describes benignly as "the commercial ebb and flow of Hollywood"[30] signals the effectiveness of the film's overriding message. Earlier in the film, after hearing gossip about Margaret being "washed up," Gretchen asks her mother: "You are a big movie star, aren't you? . . . I know you *were*, but are you now?" Margaret's assertive response is, "Well, if you're a star, you don't stop being a star." The film suggests, however, that in order to experience "just being a woman," she should.

The female star's challenge to age restrictions can also take the form of sexual transgression, as characters utilize their star status to disturb the power dynamics of male-female relations. In *The Female Animal* (Harry Keller, 1958) Hedy Lamarr's movie fame has been achieved not as an actress, but as the kind of star written about in the script being sold to Bette Davis in the conclusion of *The Star*, "the ones that play it 24 hours a day." She eases the familiarity of her Bel Air lifestyle through fleeting relationships with younger men, like the handsome extra (played by George Nader) she installs in her beach house as a "caretaker." When Lamarr assures Jan Sterling's ex–child star, bored with her own toy boy, that hers is "quite independent," Sterling makes plain the gender reversal through which these relationships function: "My dear, that's a mistake. Never let them have a career. That's the one thing I've really learned about men in Hollywood; success goes to their little heads, and one morning they're off with the car, and their gold cufflinks, and your heart, and that's that. Keep 'em sharecropping, dear, it's the only way. Tote that barge, lift that bail." Lamarr's punishment for using her stardom for sexual and economic power over her mate(s)—enslaving them, as Sterling suggests—is to have to sacrifice the man she now loves after discovering he and her daughter (played by Jane Powell) are emotionally involved.

The much more narratively complex and articulate *Sunset Boulevard* takes the theme of the older female star's sexual power further, connecting it more directly to her self-identity in relation to stardom. The famed tale of Norma Desmond, played by silent-to-sound movie star Gloria Swanson, who has been planning her return to the screen ever since the "talkies" put paid to her career, depicts a character whose inability to transcend her identity as a movie star propels her from emotional fragility to ultimate madness. Her assumption of the sexual and financial control of struggling young screenwriter Joe Gillis (played by William Holden) simultaneously becomes the site of the film's ambivalent discourse on the place of the older female star.

Much of the press around the film's release drew parallels between the careers of its protagonist and star, suggesting that both embodying the myth of stardom and displaying ambition defined the "authentic species." *Newsweek*, for example, decried the scarcity of the "glamour and authority . . . courage and industrial experience" of the kind of movie star-dom exemplified by few, citing Davis, Dietrich, Crawford, and Garbo among them. Declaring "Gloria Swanson has been a Movie Star for 32 years," the article argued her move into independent film production, the patent busi-ness, and television demonstrated that it was not she but the movie indus-try that had been left behind.[31] Wilder's referencing of Swanson and her career for the characterization of Norma is made explicit in the film's use of an extract from Swanson's 1929 film *Queen Kelly*, written and directed by Erich von Stroheim, who plays Norma's butler and first husband, Max von Mayerling, in Wilder's film. The writer-director's oft-stated longing for the kind of "authentic" movie stardom *Newsweek* describes is perhaps, however, a more palpable marker of the complexities in Norma's represen-tation. Wilder's assertion in a 1994 interview, for example, that Harrison Ford "would have been one of the crowd" in the days of Gary Cooper, Clark Gable, and Spencer Tracy indicates the reverence for a long-lost movie stardom that inhabits the narratives of *Sunset Boulevard* and its close the-matic descendant *Fedora* (Billy Wilder, 1978).[32]

The flashback structure establishing Joe's narration, the excess of both the narrative and Norma's characterization, and the representation and reception of Norma's emotional manipulation and insanity position the film in an overlapping space between film noir, melodrama, and horror. Joe's voiceover as the victim of Norma's gunshot floating as a corpse in her swimming pool establishes him as the narrator of events, privileging his perspective on Norma's character and behavior. Indeed, he suggests his aim is to relate for the audience "the facts, the whole truth" before the story is "distorted and blown out of proportion" by the Hollywood colum-nists, something we see depicted through Hedda Hopper in the final scenes. However, the narrative frequently disturbs the subjective view-point he provides, setting up a clash throughout between the film's vocal and visual representations of Norma as a star. Our first encounter with Norma's stardom, for example, is through Joe's voiceover as he recounts parking his car in the garage of her mansion while trying to escape debt collectors. Joe's description of Norma's home immediately sets up both a world and a star identity positioned in the past:

It was a great big white elephant of a place, the kind crazy movie people built in the crazy '20s. A neglected house gets an unhappy look; this one had it in spades. It was like that old woman in *Great Expectations*, that Miss Havisham in her rotting wedding dress and her torn veil, taking it out on the world because she'd been given the go-by.

When Norma appears behind the blinds of her upstairs window, thinking Joe is the mortician arrived to collect her dead monkey, she seems to be the embodiment of this relic of the more glamorous and thriving times of Hollywood's youth. Indeed, the house will become the space in which Norma's embittered nostalgia is most obviously on display. However, Joe's instant dismissal of silent movie stardom as "crazy" already vocalizes the distance between early Hollywood and its postwar counterpart that plays out in the film, with Wilder's presentation of both often acting as a corrective to Joe's unsympathetic detachment.

Joe, after all, even by his own words, seizes the opportunity to exploit Norma's desperation to return to the screen. When he first recognizes her and remarks that she "used to be in silent pictures, used to be big," it points to the contemporary industry's assumption that as a middle-aged female star Norma's career is over. Her famous response, "I *am* big. It's the pictures that got small," illustrates Norma's fundamental resistance to being "given the go-by," and her assertion that while Hollywood filmmaking artistically shrinks, her worth is tied to the excess in the mythology of old-time movie stardom.

Hollywood's decline into the commonplace, moreover, is something addressed by her plan to "return" to moviemaking. As she asserts: "Look at them in the front offices, the masterminds. They took the idols and smashed them, the Fairbankses, the Gilberts, the Valentinos. And who have we got now? Some nobodies." Norma's words echo Wilder's own later comments, illustrating the film's essential veneration of silent-movie stardom that works against Joe's narration. Moreover, Joe's manipulation of Norma so that she engages him to edit her *Salome* script that she mistakenly thinks will resurrect her career, insisting on an inflated salary and having his rent arrears paid off, indicates the deception in which Joe's narrative is founded. Indeed, he proudly admits: "I dropped the hook, and she snapped at it." As he moves into Norma's mansion, allows her to choose and pay for his clothes, and, the film obliquely suggests, provides sexual favors, Joe represents an unreliable narrator, whose subjective portrayal of himself as the victim of Norma's manipulation is ultimately tainted.

The film therefore offers two opposing perspectives on Hollywood stardom as depicted through Norma and her world. Joe expresses nothing but disdain for the myth of movie stardom. His response to Norma's diatribe against the mediocrity of sound cinema is to mock both her star status and the fandom surrounding it, suggesting he might bring his autograph book or cement for her footprints on his next visit. The bridge group of silent movie stars—played by real-life versions Buster Keaton, Anna Q. Nilsson, and H. B. Warner—Joe refers to derisively as "the waxworks," and when he imagines Mabel Normand and John Gilbert swimming in the now-empty and rat-infested pool, he exudes less nostalgia for a lost glamour than a superior distaste for the excesses of the past. Joe views Norma's home as a relic of a stardom she can no longer claim, and her attachment to it as evidence of her inability to exist outside her identity as a movie star. The surfeit of framed photographs of "her celluloid self" suggest a Norma Desmond "still waving proudly to a parade that had long since passed her by," aided by the fake fan letters sent by her director and first husband Max. In addition, Joe pointedly ties Norma's stardom to her sexuality, describing her bedroom replete with drapes and a boat-shaped bed as "the perfect setting for a silent movie queen," and thereby positioning both in historical terms. His horror on discovering her feelings for him therefore emanates from both his rejection of the myth of stardom and the artificial excess Norma represents, and his perception of her sexuality as similarly resigned to history.

Joe's narration of his story as that of a victim of Norma's emotional manipulation, sexual exploitation and economic power draws the film into horror and film noir territory, alongside the melodrama evident in Swanson's performance style and the excess of Norma's emotions, all presented as products of the silent era. Lucy Fischer therefore describes the star as "a particularly vicious character, a literal *femme fatale*," labeling her "monstrous" and a "vampire . . . waiting to ensnare her next unsuspecting victim."[33] Alan Nadel views the film as the tragic noir counterpart to *Singin' in the Rain*, with Norma's "pathetic"[34] attempt to assume power over her career in a "ghoulish unearthing of the past"[35] putting a dark spin on Lina Lamont's transgressive stardom. The unreliability of Joe's narration, however, challenges such readings of Norma's star identity, particularly in the context of the film's depiction of contemporary Hollywood. Silent and sound cinema are undoubtedly set against each other, with Joe's disdain for Hollywood's past confronted by both Wilder's delight in movie stardom and his portrayal of an uninspiring new film industry. Norma's dramatic performance of her star identity in her emotional and physical world of excess suggests a stardom that is obsolete. Simultaneously, such glamorous overplaying references the essential extraordinariness upon which star mythology is founded, and which the film partially celebrates in Norma.

In contrast, contemporary Hollywood is depicted as an unimaginative business where Paramount producer Sheldrake turns down *Gone with the Wind* (Victor Fleming, 1939) and hunts for star vehicles for Betty Hutton, and Joe's agent spends his days in Bel Air "making with the golf sticks." Moreover, while Joe and budding screenwriter Betty Schaefer (played by Nancy Olson) spend their time at a New Year's Eve party ridiculing the formulaic melodrama of Hollywood's genre filmmaking in a mock scene, Norma's displays of star quality highlight the blandness of the current era's inhabitants, accentuated by Betty's claim to prefer a career behind the screen after the studio passed on her as a prospective movie star. Joe's narrated boredom at having to watch Norma perform routines as a Mack Sennett bathing beauty and Charlie Chaplin, and our discomfort at the context of their now-sexual relationship initiated by her threats to kill herself, are disturbed by the evidence that the performances provide of Norma's charismatic value. In the same way, when Norma runs one of her silent movies as proof of "what a star looks like," Wilder's use of Swanson's 1929 film *Queen Kelly* (also directed by von Stroheim) is not solely a further display of the egotism that partly defines Norma, but a visual reinforcement of her assertions about stardom through the scene's reminder that the clearest identifier of star charisma in the stardom narrative is screen performance. Standing in a literal spotlight, Norma's declaration—"I'll be up there again, so help me."—is therefore not only a statement of personal ambition, but also a move to replace the conventional with the spectacular.

Norma's attempt to bring the mansion back to life by restoring the pool and dancing on the floor once occupied by Valentino symbolizes her attempt to renew her star status in the present. Max's well-meaning subterfuge has convinced them both that Norma "*is* the greatest star of them all," and the film affirms her argument that "We didn't need dialogue, we had faces." However, Norma's mistake is both her failure to recognize that voices are now as important as faces, and her assumption that a male-dominated industry will sanction her return (she hates the word "come-back," which assumes the resurrection of a failed career). When she returns to Paramount Studios to see another of her former directors, Cecil B. DeMille (playing himself), under the false impression of his interest in her *Salome* screenplay, the repeated comment "I thought she was dead" emanating from the sound stage of *Samson and Delilah* (Cecil B. DeMille, 1949) indicates how the industry views an older female star.

As she bats away an intrusive microphone, pointing to her disdain for sound cinema, she nevertheless returns to an identity that combines a creative worker with a bona fide movie star. The warmth with which the old-time extras gather to greet her suggests a Hollywood community, just as Hog-eye's direction of a spotlight on Norma becomes another occasion when her worth as a star is explicitly recognized. DeMille's response, however, punctures this scene as his superficial affection for Norma becomes condescension when he schools her, "You know, pictures have changed quite a bit," as well as cold dismissal as he instructs Hog-eye to "Turn that light back where it belongs" (figure 2.6). More than a statement, Norma's plea is "I just want to work again," and contrasts with DeMille's apparently seamless transition from silent to sound as a male director. Like her luxurious car, the Isotta-Fraschini that the studio wants to hire for a Bing Crosby movie, her stardom is viewed as little more than a fascinating curiosity of the past; the reemergence of her ego when she reminds DeMille, "I don't work before 10.00 in the morning, and never after 4.30 in the afternoon," seems, then, to reaffirm her poor fit in this new Hollywood.

Despite the emotional disturbance we witness in Norma's suicide attempt, the mental instability with which Joe associates her is narrated retrospectively through the narrative's flashback framing and comes to fruition only in the film's concluding scenes. Indeed, Wilder and co-screenwriter Charles Brackett had amended an early version of the script when the characterization of Norma seemed to veer too far toward insanity, Brackett noting in his diaries their intent to write Norma as "a rich egocentric woman" rather than as "a madwoman."[36] The combination of being confronted by Joe's deception and the fact that her stardom is now an illusion reveals her emotional breakdown in the final scenes when she shoots and kills Joe and the press "hoop-de-do" that Joe has predicted is

Fig. 2.6: *Sunset Boulevard* (Paramount, 1950). The spotlight shines again on Norma Desmond (Gloria Swanson), if only temporarily.

unveiled. Only at this point does Joe express some sympathy for Norma, as the voiceover and visual representation of Norma merge to elevate stardom above the venality of the press and media industries. As we watch Hedda Hopper phone in her copy in the bedroom where the police are interviewing Norma Desmond in the throes of insanity, Joe imagines the fatal blow of headlines like "Forgotten Star a Slayer" and "Ageing Actress." The newsreel cameras rolling for a fictional scene of Max's creation, however, enable the film's depiction of the kind of "happy madness"[37] that was intended for Norma, and as she moves into the spotlight for a close-up, the film leaves us with an image of stardom that the industry of the narrative had failed to provide.

Horror and Historical Drama

What Ever Happened to Baby Jane? (Robert Aldrich, 1962) moves the balance between melodrama and horror more clearly into the latter, most obviously due to its underpinning of excess and performance represented around aging femininity and stardom. The connections made in the film's narrative between the aging female body, violence, and the loss of stardom suggest that its horror lies in the refusal to acknowledge a definition of stardom bound up in youth, sexuality, and glamour. At the same time, Bette Davis's repeated association with the characterization of female stardom in decline, alongside her frank public pronouncements on Hollywood's treatment of older female stars, disrupts the positioning of mature femininity as monstrous and its stars as deluded, just as the performance of acting becomes its own challenge to the narrative theme.

The film's narrative structure establishes the theme of unruly female stardom in its pre-credit opening prologue set in 1917 when vaudeville child star Baby Jane Hudson (Davis) exhibits the obnoxious behavior that embodies the idea of the spoilt child star represented in films such as *Kathy O'* (Jack Sher, 1958). The contrast between the affable stage performer and the insufferable child revealed to fans at the stage door, demanding ice cream because "I make the money so I can have what I want," immediately positions Jane as both grotesque and transgressive for the narrative events that will occur. The scene equally reinforces the constructed nature of performance and its economic imperative through the Baby Jane replica dolls promoted onstage and sold in the lobby by her accompanist and manager father.

The narrative at this point therefore sets the character premise for sister Blanche's (Joan Crawford) assertion that Jane is responsible for the car accident that leaves Blanche paralyzed. Jane's later abusive behavior all but erases young Blanche's pledge that she won't forget the poor treatment meted out to her by the family's performers, which hints at the jealousy that is, in fact, responsible for both the accident and what follows and revealed only in the narrative's final twist.

These scenes additionally serve to introduce the notion of unruliness around Jane, which is reinforced in the second prologue set in 1935, where Jane's agent and a Hollywood producer discuss how Jane's drinking and partying has been hushed up by the studio for the sake of Blanche's blossoming career. Jane's unruliness will later be conveyed through her slovenly appearance as she drinks and shuffles around the house, the psychological disturbance evident in her poor treatment of Blanche, her desire evident in her attempt at a relationship with a younger man, and her unwillingness to accept the past nature of her stardom, all unruliness that suggests resistance to accepted notions of femininity and to the entertainment industry's definition of female stardom. Through the characterization of each of these elements as excess, Jane is defined as a "monstrous" version of femininity as it transitions into middle age, and of female stardom as it fails to submit to control or to acknowledge its limited lifespan.

The film's depiction of an ex-vaudeville child star and failed Hollywood actress keeping her paralyzed movie star sister hostage in their decaying home paints an horrific picture of emotional and physical abuse, as does the final revelation that Blanche had attempted to murder her sister and is the cause of her psychological breakdown. As such, *What Ever Happened to Baby Jane?* might be considered as part of a series of horror films of the 1960s and 1970s starring some of the female stars of Hollywood's studio era, which represent a shift of genre from the woman's film or melodrama to horror. Olivia de Havilland in *Lady in a Cage* (Walter Grauman, 1964) and Lana Turner in *Persecution* (Don Chaffey, 1974), for example, represent this shifting career trajectory, embodied more forcefully in the later careers of the stars of *Baby Jane*. Both stars initially followed the production with *Hush . . . Hush, Sweet Charlotte* (1964), again under the direction of Robert Aldrich, although Crawford was replaced by de Havilland after some initial filming due to a fractious set and Crawford's extended sick leave. Films such as *The Nanny* (Seth Holt, 1965) add to Davis's association with the genre, just as Crawford's appearances in the increasingly exploitative *Strait-Jacket* (William Castle, 1964), *Berserk* (Jim O'Connolly, 1967), and *Trog* (Freddie Francis, 1970) gave the impression of an industry almost delighting in its destruction of the myth of the glamorous female star, something to which the later miniseries *Feud: Bette and Joan* (FX, 2017) explicitly refers.

The film's depiction of the characters as decaying versions of their younger selves as stars therefore seems mirrored by the star identities of Davis and Crawford on display, even close-ups of Crawford appearing to cruelly illuminate the older face that in her youth would have been lit to convey a glamorous perfection. This contrasting and mirroring process becomes explicit in the use of Davis and Crawford films within the narrative; Davis's *Parachute Jumper* (Alfred E. Green, 1933) is screened for Blanche's agent Marty (played by Wesley Addy) and studio producer Ben (played by Bert Freed) as narrative evidence of Jane's lack of screen-acting ability, and Crawford's *Sadie McKee* (Clarence Brown, 1934) is watched by both Blanche and her neighbors on daytime television, the daughter (played by Davis's own daughter B.D.) musing that Blanche must be 150.

What the film represents as a grotesque deterioration of female beauty, however, simultaneously exposes the performativity inherent in the presentation of femininity and female stardom. Anne Morey explains: "The grotesque, in other words, recalls the vulnerability already latent even in women's most youthful roles, and thus demonstrates the omnipresence of effort in constructing femininity from youth to age, for the star and the celebrity."[38] Moreover, Davis's renown as a movie star concerned less with glamour than with the display of acting skills intervenes in the notion of a film's representation of a passive star as well as their characterization. In films including *Of Human Bondage* (John Cromwell, 1934), *Now, Voyager* (Irving Rapper, 1942), *Mr. Skeffington* (Vincent Sherman, 1944), and *The Virgin Queen* (Henry Koster, 1955), Davis is depicted on screen in ways unusual for a leading female star of the studio system, indicating her prioritization of the service of character and narrative. Throughout her career, Davis not only asserted her willingness to appear physically unattractive on-screen, but also actively disrupted studio attempts to package her as a female star—for example, by reverting to her natural hair color against studio instructions after Warner Bros. had dyed it blonde.[39] When the adult Jane sings and dances to her child star theme, "I've written a letter to daddy," observes herself in the mirror, and bursts into tears, therefore, the scene conveys Jane's horror at her physical deterioration and loss of star status, and, in opposition, emphasizes Davis's embodiment of such beauty-defying artistry.

The series of films in which Davis confronts Hollywood's insistence that older female stars vanish from the screen, in addition, creates an essential ambivalence.[40] The film therefore veers between displaying Jane's female form as a shadow of its former self—articulated through the excess of her white make-up, slovenly appearance and lifeless feet-dragging, at times all contained within the incongruity of a child's costume—and displaying the performance of culturally required femininity. At the same time, Jane's continuous refusal to disappear following her success as a child star, attempting both an early Hollywood career and a present-day return to the stage, alongside Davis's embodiment of persistence in her screen and star image, represents a combined challenge to such social and cultural attitudes to aging femininity and stardom.

The film's ambivalence toward the longevity of stardom is pervasive in the film. As the neighbors watch television transfixed by Blanche's early film, and Jane discards fan letters sent to Blanche that are evidence of a new generation of fans created by television re-runs, the film points to the potency of stardom on the screen. Jane, however, notably attempts to retrieve the stardom she enjoyed as a child star on the vaudeville stage rather than revisiting her failed Hollywood career. When local grifter Edwin (played by Victor Buono) responds to her newspaper advertisement for a pianist to accompany her in the nightclub appearances she imagines coming to fruition, and his audition becomes an opportunity for her to perform in full costume, his looks of dismay despite his insincere praise recognize the fantasy of Jane's plans that Edwin will attempt to exploit (figure 2.7). The sisters' active participation in the creation of their stardom, therefore,

Fig. 2.7: Baby Jane Hudson refuses to resign her childhood stardom to the past in *What Ever Happened to Baby Jane?* (Warner Bros., 1962).

remains confined to the past, with the sisters instead ensconced in the former home of Rudolph Valentino, an additional symbol of fame's ability to both endure and settle within a dormant past.

The critical reception of *Baby Jane* mirrored the narrative's ambivalent depiction of aging female stardom. Describing the film as a "flood of sheer grotesquerie," Bosley Crowther of the *New York Times* poured cold water on the idea that it was an exercise in artistry, suggesting, "[W]e're afraid this unique conjunction of the two one-time top-ranking stars in a story about two ageing sisters who were once theatrical celebrities themselves does not afford either opportunity to do more than wear grotesque costumes, make-up to look like witches and chew the scenery to shreds."[41] James Powers in the *Hollywood Reporter*, on the other hand, termed *Baby Jane* "a high-class horror film, in the Hitchcock vein" and delivered praise to both actresses, commenting, "Miss Davis plays with all the baroque technique at her command, which is unmatched by any other actress" and "Miss Crawford plays her scenes of cajolery, panic and despair with supple skill."[42] The stars themselves were wary of critical and audience responses to the film, Crawford refusing to join Davis on the publicity tour and Davis famously posting an advertisement in *Variety* pitching herself as an actor for hire in order to pre-empt what she feared would be another flop, even though Davis later insisted the action was taken "tongue-in-cheek."[43]

Commenting upon the insecure market for female stardom in the context of the film's box-office and critical success, however, highlighted the incongruous nature of Hollywood's perception of the economic value of female stars. In interviews publicizing the film, Davis continuously drew attention to the studios' resistance to financing a movie with middle-aged female stars as its central protagonists. As she told television host Jack Paar, she and Crawford felt justified in feeling "a little gloaty" at their ability to confound the expectations of industry men whose initial response to the project had been "Those two old broads? I wouldn't give you a dime."[44] Davis, in turn, embraced her renewed stardom, singing the film's title song and dancing amongst a troupe of showboys on the *Andy Williams Show*,[45] as well as viewing the film's success as an opportunity to reassert herself as a significant artistic force. Visiting the Cannes Film Festival with *Baby Jane* in 1963, where the *New York Times* reported, "At every public appearance, Miss Davis was mobbed by fans, autograph hunters and photographers," she told one interviewer the film represented her fight to once again become "an important contributor to the industry I love the most."[46] Davis's direct expression of her own struggle to maintain stardom in middle age within the Hollywood system reinforces *Baby Jane*'s implicit critique of the limitations placed on female stardom by Hollywood past and present.

While two remakes of *What Ever Happened to Baby Jane?* appeared—an ABC television version in 1991 starring Redgrave sisters Vanessa and Lynn (an obvious nod to their relationship as sisters and actors), and a short-lived 2002 musical staged in Houston—the West End play *Bette & Joan*, which ran in 2011, focused on the production of the film and the contentious relationship between the two stars. The famed enmity between them had been raised continuously in the press during production and in reviews of the film, as well as most comprehensively in Shaun Considine's book *Bette & Joan: The Divine Feud*, a clear, if unacknowledged, source for Ryan Murphy's FX anthology series *Feud: Bette and Joan*—starring Jessica Lange and Susan Sarandon—which aired in the United States in 2017.

Following the genesis of *What Ever Happened to Baby Jane?* as a project, through its production and release, and past the subsequent filming of *Hush . . . Hush, Sweet Charlotte* and Crawford's dismissal from the film, the series treads familiar territory. Detailing the professional rivalries and personal animosity between the stars, the various episodes utilize a fair amount of poetic license asserted as evidenced fact in their focus on the gossipy aspects of the stars' significance in relation to *Baby Jane*, building on the tell-all family histories published by both stars' daughters and, most famously, the film version of Christina Crawford's book, *Mommie Dearest* (Frank Perry, 1981).[47] Olivia de Havilland, moreover, attempted without success to take a lawsuit as far as the Supreme Court against what she viewed as the show's misrepresentation of her character through unverified storytelling.

The show's other core focus, however, is the film industry's treatment of older female stars, dismissing them at a certain age as damaged relics of a glamorous Hollywood history, or past their financial worth as stars able to ensure box-office returns. Further, it depicts a system in which studio heads like Jack Warner readily promote antipathy between female stars for the purposes of publicity. By doing so, however, the series by default accepts the notion that the horror genre was a professional demotion for the stars of *Baby Jane*. While Crawford's identity as an icon of Hollywood glamour is, at the very least, disrupted by these films, Davis's image constructed around skilled artistry and an anti-glamour approach means that *Baby Jane* and her subsequent role as the emotionally troubled and victimized Charlotte might equally suggest a determined claim to continued stardom.

The hybridity inherent in the stardom narrative as it merges with a variety of genres produces diverse representations of the movie star myth, as generic forms and themes intervene to bring added layers of meaning to these films. Their association, particularly with the musical, melodrama, film noir, and horror, with the additional generic overlaps that occur, constructs differing depictions of model movie stardom that display everything from idealization, to disruptive critique and confused ambivalence. The films that follow explore stardom in ways that reveal a similar layering of mythology, as boundaries are blurred between the past and the present, star and character, and fact and fiction, and the stardom narrative confronts the inescapable nature of its own myth.

3   CHARACTER, STAR, AND MYTH

In the 2002 film *Simone* (Andrew Niccol), Al Pacino plays a Hollywood producer who relieves his frustrations at the power of movie stars exemplified by Winona Ryder's unruly actress by creating a computer-generated version of stardom. When the fictional image he builds in the likeness of studio stars like Audrey Hepburn again assumes control, however, and the producer is accused of the star's "murder," the creation of a virtual baby becomes necessary in order to reassert the realness of the unreal. In *The Purple Rose of Cairo* (Woody Allen, 1985) and *Last Action Hero* (John McTiernan, 1993), movie stars and audiences move between the real world and the movie world, as fans play characters on the screen and stars shed their stardom to escape and become "real" people. Each of these films blurs the boundaries between the on- and offscreen worlds and the movie star and the audience, suggesting the mythical and the real as overlapping concepts. These contemporary films revisit tropes established in early examples of Hollywood self-reflection. Buster Keaton's movie projectionist in *Sherlock Jr.* (Buster Keaton, 1924), for example, becomes the hero of his own story as he passes through and onto the screen as the detective who resolves the crime and so restores his relationship.[1] Earlier, in the silent Keystone Productions short *Mabel's Dramatic Career* (previously mentioned in relation to the escape narrative), young farmhand Mack Sennett chases his ex-fiancée (played by Mabel Normand) to the city unaware of her new identity as a movie star. When he sees her in the grasp of a

Keystone villain, he attempts to save her by shooting at the screen, unable to distinguish between the real world and its fictional counterpart. His continued confusion on spying the actor at home with Normand's movie star and their children results in a second attempt to shoot, thwarted only by a neighbor pouring a bucket of water over the out-of-towner's head.

These films display the powerful effects of the myth of Hollywood stardom, such that it continuously crosses the boundaries between worlds and realities. Fans can literally will themselves onto the screen and become movie stars; movie star characters are real in the audience's world, or, alternatively, exist as computer-generated constructions as long as the myth is believable. This chapter explores how stardom films address the blurring of boundaries in a variety of ways that are often less stark than these examples. As movie stars play fictional and real movie star characters, narratives draw on earlier incarnations of stardom, and the constructed nature of imagery circulates thematically alongside the myths of the gods, the films question distinctions between reality and myth and explore stardom mythology and its representation as necessarily multilayered.

Ghosts of Stardom

Prefacing the 1952 comedy *Dreamboat* (Claude Binyon) in which university professor and ex–silent movie star Clifton Webb is lured onto television by his former co-star played by Ginger Rogers, *Callaway Went Thataway* (Norman Panama and Melvin Frank, 1951) plays with the theme of the reemergence of a star identity prompted by the screening of old movies on television. When the westerns of Smoky Callaway (played by Howard Keel) become a television hit, two marketing executives for the advertising agency sponsoring the show, played by Fred MacMurray and Dorothy McGuire, seek out the Hollywood "has-been" in an attempt to exploit his career revival. Unable to locate him and instead finding an actual cowboy who happens to be a doppelganger for Callaway, they pass off the fake version as the real one until Callaway reemerges. When the small-time movie star turns out to be a self-centered drunk, while the cowboy sets up a youth foundation with his financial rewards, the film suggests the off-screen version of a western hero better represents the onscreen myth than does the star originally constructed by Hollywood. A scene in which the two characters (both played by Keel) appear on screen together further questions who might assume the status of the "real" mythological star (figure 3.1). The film's coda, in turn, seeks to reassert star mythology by reassuring its audience that the film "meant in no way to detract from the wholesome influence, civic mindedness and the many charitable contributions of Western idols of our American youth, or to be a portrayal of any of them."

The theme of the ghost of a mythological stardom located in the past runs through stardom narratives, as films look to and construct earlier representations of stardom and confront its layered mythology. Echoes of *Sunset Boulevard* reverberate in a number of these films, including the third in the Robert Aldrich trilogy centered on the theme of stardom that followed *The Big Knife* and *What Ever Happened to Baby Jane?*. *The Legend of Lylah Clare* (1968) features Kim Novak, drawing on the duality of her roles as Madeline and Judy in *Vertigo* (Alfred Hitchcock, 1958). The dead woman's image that dominates *Vertigo*'s narrative shifts from Hitchcock's painting of Carlotta Valdes to the cinematic image of movie star Lylah Clare, the

Fig. 3.1: *Callaway Went Thataway* (MGM, 1951). Who is the "real" western hero?

wife of director Lewis Zarkan, played by Peter Finch. When Zarkan is alerted to the striking resemblance Novak's actress Elsa Campbell (born Brinkmann) bears to Lylah (also played by Novak in flashback), he attempts to resurrect Lylah as a star via a biopic starring Elsa.

The mystery of Lylah's death pervades the film (three versions are presented via flashbacks), while Zarkan and Lylah's lesbian lover Rossella (played by Rossella Falk) live in a decaying mansion saturated with photographs of the dead star and "consume her memory after death."[2] Lylah's bedroom remains unchanged since the couple's wedding day, a further reference to Joe Gillis's description of Norma Desmond's home evoking a modern-day *Great Expectations*, and to *Sunset Boulevard*'s allusion to a brand of stardom long since departed. A *Life* magazine cover story features Elsa as a "Live Ghost in an Enchanted Cemetery," pointing to the blurred lines the film suggests between the idealized image of a dead star and the actress who will embody her life on the screen. As Elsa becomes possessed by Lylah's identity, speaking periodically in a deep, guttural voice and German accent, Aldrich returns to the theme of monstrous female stardom associated with the reemergence of an image that exists in the past.

The agency here, however, is not that of the literally dead star, nor of her live embodiment, despite Elsa's attempt to rewrite Lylah's story in the biopic's final scene (or, alternatively, Lylah, now fully embodied by Elsa) by assuming the role of the director. Indeed, Zarkan asserts: "We make the legend. The legend becomes the truth." As Elsa becomes consumed by the ghost of a star image and falls to her death while Zarkan keeps the cameras rolling, the film represents a literal illustration of Hollywood's belief in the primacy of the imaginary over the real, even as the on-screen and off-screen stories of both stars merge. The industry's celebration of the director's efforts, however, suggests the film's coda of a television dog food commercial that concludes with a ravaging pack of dogs offers a corrective to the narrative's often confused and limited critique, as cinematic artistry is set against consumerist television.

A more effective treatise on the illusory nature of star mythology occurs in *Fedora*, in which Billy Wilder revisits the theme of lost stardom. Drawing explicitly on *Sunset Boulevard*, the film emphasizes the essential construct of image in a narrative that continues to carry an aura of the ghost of a Hollywood past and passed. Adopting one of Wilder's key tropes of role-playing and disguise, *Fedora* simultaneously examines the ruinous effects of Hollywood's fixation on youth and beauty on the female star. In the October 1969 issue of *Cinema*, Robert Mundy identified the connection between role-playing and disguise in the director's films, suggesting, "Disguises are metaphors for roles in Wilder's films, and his protagonists change disguises." The adoption, rejection, and performance of roles, and the attendant images acting to disguise reality, therefore, frequently become part of both character transformation and narrative theme.[3] *Fedora* explores image construction in its native locale amongst stars as the ultimate role-players, dramatizing the literal displacement of a star by an image.

The narrative centers on Polish-born Hollywood star Fedora (played by Hildegard Knef), who retires from the screen after one of her regular bouts of plastic surgery leaves her face permanently scarred and she is confined to a wheelchair after a resulting stroke. Retreating to seclusion in the Greek Islands on the pretense of an early retirement, Fedora finds her stardom resurrected when the Academy of Motion Picture Arts and Sciences bestows on her a Special Oscar, delivered in person by the Academy's president, Henry Fonda (as himself), which Fedora's daughter, Antonia (played by Marthe Keller), accepts in disguise as her mother. In order to take advantage of the movie offers that follow press photographs of the event, Antonia permanently assumes Fedora's identity, undergoing a physical transformation and performing the role of actress and star, while her mother takes on a disguise as her lover's deceased mother, Countess Sobryanski, concealing herself à la Norma Desmond in her mausoleum of a mansion. When Antonia is eventually confronted by the realization that she can never regain her own identity, she commits suicide, jumping into the path of an incoming train, thus suggesting to the world the death of Fedora.

The story is framed around two flashbacks, the first narrated by independent film producer Barry "Dutch" Detweiler, played by William Holden, and the second by Fedora/Countess Sobryanski. Holden's casting makes clear reference to Wilder's earlier Hollywood fable, signaling both the character's direct connection to Hollywood's studio era and the unreliability of his protagonist's narration. As he observes the fans, journalists and cameramen attending Fedora's lying-in-state, so carefully stage-managed by the Countess that he likens it to a film premiere, Detweiler relates what he believes to be a true version of the events of the previous two weeks. His voyage to Corfu has been an attempt to secure Fedora's services for a version of *Anna Karenina* he is producing entitled "The Snows of Yesteryear" (the former a tale that ends with the protagonist throwing herself in the path of a train), aiming to trade on the brief affair they had when he was an assistant director on one of her Hollywood films. The illusory quality of his encounters with Fedora and the Countess is revealed, however, when the Countess unmasks herself as Fedora and relates the story of her disfigurement, her self-imposed exile from the screen, and the reconstruction of the star image of "Fedora" through her daughter (figure 3.2). The Countess's scheme is on a grand scale and, while extinguishing her daughter's identity and ultimately her life, achieves its goal of maintaining "Fedora's" stardom through the construction of an improbably youthful version of the star. The film industry's obsession with youth and a star's visual appeal provides a rationale for such behavior, which accounts for Fedora's initial cosmetic procedures and her willingness to transform her daughter in her own image. When her aide, Miss Balfour, comments that Antonia failed to match her mother as an actress, the Countess responds: "Aaah, acting.

Fig. 3.2: The performed identities of mother (Hildegard Knef) and daughter (Marthe Keller) in *Fedora* (United Artists, 1978).

That's for the Old Vic, but every so often a face comes along the camera falls in love with. You're born with that." The obvious reference to Norma Desmond's assertion—"We had faces."—carries with it the irony that Antonia achieves stardom in disguise via a reconstructed version of Fedora's face, one with which neither was therefore born.

Nevertheless, the faux Fedora's flourishing career and the audience and press response to her death all validate the "real" Fedora's assumptions about the industry's approach to stardom, as the crowds flock for a last glance at the face in the coffin, unaware of the extent to which this face—reconstructed again following Antonia's suicide—is a mere image. This critique of the hollowness of the myth is marked by ambivalence expressed through Detweiler, who rails at a Hollywood film industry financially controlled by "tax shelter guys" and the "kids with beards" who now direct, suggesting a New Hollywood update to *Sunset Boulevard*'s criticism of the "idiot producers" and "message kids." Talking to the *Los Angeles Times* during production of the church sequences in Paris, Wilder drew attention to the shifting industry context of a financially insecure Hollywood and increasing European production in which *Fedora* was being made, illuminating parallels with the international search for investment undertaken by his narrator: "[T]he old days we would have brought Cherbourg to Santa Monica . . . Now we bring Santa Monica to Cherbourg because that's where the money is."[4]

Wilder's comments on the casting of the film, alongside the elevation of silent movie stardom in *Sunset Boulevard*, similarly frame the thematic approach in *Fedora*. Explaining his initial intention to cast Marlene Dietrich as the Countess and Faye Dunaway as the new Fedora, before an unsuccessful attempt to have Marthe Keller play both roles, Wilder lamented again the disappearance of an earlier era of stars: "I have known Garbo, Swanson, Dietrich, Lombard, and Monroe . . . and today there is nobody like them left in Hollywood. Fedora is not based on any of them; she is a fictitious combination of them all, and it is difficult for a young actress to play such a part."[5] A reviewer for the *New Republic* concurred that the role was "nowadays, impossible to cast."[6] In another intervention into the film's blurred layers of myth and reality, Wilder reported that Dietrich rejected the role with a sense that it mirrored too closely her own life. His character Detweiler's reference to the loss of stars like Gable, Tracy, and Crawford, and the Countess's receipt of a letter of condolence from

Dietrich, whom she terms "a real fighter," expresses Wilder's yearning for an epoch of Hollywood stardom that the film suggests now exists only in the fake form of a wholly constructed identity. Henry Fonda's appearance as himself—an aging star—moreover, and his lack of surprise at Fedora's youthful appearance, serve as a reminder of the more realistic expectations of youth and beauty placed on a male star. The Countess's awareness that "Fedora's" renewed stardom required conformity to the movie star ideal therefore forms a validating backdrop to her attempt to recreate her own myth. As she explains: "People were tired of what passes for entertainment these days. Cinéma vérité, the naked truth, the uglier the better. They wanted glamour again, and who was I to disappoint them?"

A number of reviewers drew attention to parallels with the exploration of myth in John Ford's 1962 western *The Man Who Shot Liberty Valance* summarized in its famous line of dialogue: "This is the West, sir. When the legend becomes fact, print the legend." Stephen Farber, for example, commented:

> Both Ford and Wilder see that the legends people create are too potent and seductive to be subverted by the truth. The difference between Liberty Valance and Fedora is that Ford celebrates the creation of a legend while Wilder protests the dire consequences of surrendering to legend. For Fedora is a horror story about lives that are destroyed by the pressure of keeping up the façade, the image, the myth; it's about the people who are sacrificed to the ravenous ego of the superstar.[7]

The metaphorical and literal deaths that occur in *Fedora*, as well as its association with both *Sunset Boulevard* and *What Ever Happened to Baby Jane?* and their representations of the hidden, aging female star, suggest elements of the horror to which Farber refers. The film points less to "ravenous ego," though, than to the tragedy of a modern myth of the West wherein the dominance of image means identity, reality, and, ultimately, life itself are overwhelmed. Yet image retains its fascination as the narrative concludes. Revealing herself to Detweiler as the "real" Fedora, the Countess nevertheless maintains her performance and the constructed identity of "Fedora" for a funeral that is actually that of her daughter, Antonia. As adoring audiences worship the reconstructed image of a woman

Fig. 3.3: *Fedora* (United Artists, 1978). "They wanted glamour again, and who was I to disappoint them?"

they mistakenly believe to be their beloved movie star Fedora lying in state, Detweiler describes the event as "going out in style, what with the spotlights, and the fiddlers, and the honour guard with feathers in their helmets, and all those TV cameras, like it was some goddamn premiere" (figure 3.3). The dissolve between the real and the fictional again finds its most potent space on the screen, repeating the imaginary production of Norma Desmond's final scene. All that remains, the film suggests, is the image. As the Countess tells Detweiler: "Endings are very important. That's what people remember — the last exit, the final close-up."

Veiled Biopics

Alongside narratives haunted by the myth of a fictional star are those in which the texts of real Hollywood stars seep into the narratives, intervening in the space between character and star image. Explicitly referential to the reported lives and identities of stars while presented as wholly fictional works, these veiled biopics acknowledge the strong presence of (actual) Hollywood movie stars in the exploration of the star myth within the genre and establish the link to star biopics. Writer-director Joseph

Mankiewicz's 1954 film *The Barefoot Contessa*, originally entitled "Rain for the Contessa," stars Ava Gardner as Maria Vargas, a Spanish dancer transported from a club in the backstreets of Madrid to Hollywood. When stardom isolates her and restricts her freedom, she attempts to escape through a stream of unsatisfying relationships and is eventually murdered by her Italian nobleman husband, the only man she has loved.

Mankiewicz's intent to create a film drawing on the culture and personnel of contemporary Hollywood is evident in an early version of the screenplay in which the character of the Hollywood producer, later known as Kirk Edwards, is referred to as Joe Schenck, the head of production at 20th Century Fox at the time of the film's production, with a later addition suggesting "COMBINE J.S. and H.H." explained in handwriting as "Joe Schenck and Howard Hughes."[8] The film's narrative has often been viewed as a thinly veiled biopic of Rita Hayworth due to elements of the narrative that seem to replicate Hayworth's life story, including Maria's Spanish dancer roots, her personal contract with an autocratic producer, and her marriage to European royalty. Hayworth, in turn, was born in Brooklyn but performed as a dancer with her Spanish father, Eduardo Cansino, was contracted to Columbia and reportedly subjected to the tyranny and abuse of studio head Harry Cohn, and was married for the third time in 1949 to Prince Aly Kahn. In *Ava: My Story*, Gardner's posthumous autobiography compiled from her personal tapes, Gardner too suggested Hayworth was the film's subject, although a later biography indicates the star claimed the script was based on her own life.[9] There seems no evidence other than rumor that Mankiewicz drew specifically from Hayworth's life. *Newsweek* in October 1954 was already debunking such claims, commenting that "columnists have reported that this romantic roulade about Maria Vargas (played by Ava Gardner) was fashioned after the life of Rita Hayworth. This is wishful thinking on somebody's part."[10]

The film appears, in fact, to draw more explicitly on imagery surrounding Gardner, although she was not the only star in the running for the role. In a seeming desire to engage in some star-making of his own, Mankiewicz was initially in favor of casting an outsider, suggesting of the film in correspondence with his casting director: "It cannot help but bring immediate stardom to whoever plays it."[11] He initially considered the inexperienced Libyan actress Rossana Podestà, who had not yet made a Hollywood film, while simultaneously suggesting, "Ideally, she should be a Spanish gypsy dancer who can act."[12] Correspondence during the scriptwriting stage between Mankiewicz and William Morris agent Bert Allenberg indicates that Jean Simmons was being pushed by Allenberg as a strong casting option, alongside mentions of Susan Hayward and Jennifer Jones.[13] However, after dismissing the idea of an unknown, Mankiewicz's inclination certainly seems to have been to focus on Gardner. Throughout both the writing and casting processes quiet discussions were taking place with MGM's Benny Thau following what Mankiewicz confirms was Nicholas Schenck's refusal to agree to the loan-out of Gardner due to an earlier confrontation between the two men.[14] Resistant to Simmons's requests for reassurance about her ability to take on the role, and learning of Allenberg's attempts to work out possible scheduling issues with the more amenable Thau, Mankiewicz stressed in a letter to the agent dated July 14, 1953: "I am most, *most* anxious to hear about Ava Gardner."[15] Further letters in October from Allenberg indicate Gardner's enthusiasm for the project, in part due to the breakdown of her marriage to Frank Sinatra fueling her desire for work overseas. The agent reported that "Ava has now become so violently rabid to do it that she said she would tear down the walls in the studio if it could not be arranged."[16]

The film follows the story of the fictional Maria Vargas, initially a Spanish dancer of renown in the locale of the tavernas of Madrid. The arrival of a Hollywood posse consisting of writer-director Harry Dawes (played by Humphrey Bogart), publicity man Oscar Muldoon (played by Edmond O'Brien), and Wall Street financier and wannabe Hollywood producer Kirk Edwards (played by Warren Stevens), with put-upon starlet in tow (played by Mari Aldon), sets in train Vargas's transformation into Hollywood star Maria D'Amata. This establishing scenario draws on contemporaneous industry strategies to counteract the studios' postwar financial decline and Hollywood stars' increasing desire for independence by cultivating talent located overseas, particularly in Europe. The chapters of Maria's life proceed from Spanish dancer, to movie star under personal contract to Edwards, to reluctant consort to a South American millionaire, to the bride of an impotent Italian nobleman, relayed through a series of flashbacks. Each chapter, including the film's opening scene, commences in the Italian graveyard hosting Maria's funeral, connecting the present day to the past through the voiceover narration of, foremost, Bogart's Dawes, but also of Muldoon and Maria's husband, Count Vincenzo Torlato-Favrini, played by Rossano Brazzi. This funereal setting frames Maria's passage through stardom with an inevitable sense of doom realized by the narrative in each chapter, and points again to the theme of death—careers, identities, lives—which permeates the genre's exploration of myth. The statue of Maria, based on her final identity as the Countess Torlato-Favrini, which dominates the graveyard scene, simultaneously emphasizes the film's deconstruction of the mythology of movie deity and how this plays out through the screen image of Ava Gardner.

Rita Hayworth, tagged by the press a "love goddess" during World War II, was closely associated with the image of Hollywood stars as the gods and goddesses of the movie screen made flesh. In *Down to Earth* (Alexander Hall, 1947), Hayworth played the goddess Terpsichore, exchanging the heavens for Earth to show the producer of a Broadway musical (played by Larry Parks) how to represent the Muses with appropriate respect. The title of the 1983 television biopic starring *Wonder Woman* (ABC/CBS, 1975–79) actress Lynda Carter, *Rita Hayworth: The Love Goddess* (James Goldstone), indicates her continuing identification with this kind of explicit imagery. Ava Gardner's image, however, is even more potently infused with goddess mythology, both on the screen and off. *The Barefoot Contessa* is the third film that ties Gardner to the figure of the mythical goddess, following, initially, *One Touch of Venus* (William A. Seiter, 1948), in which she plays a department store statue that becomes the living embodiment of the goddess Venus brought to life by a kiss from Robert Walker's window dresser. In *Pandora and the Flying Dutchman* (Albert Lewin, 1951), her character's image is drawn into posterity as the "darling of the gods" through the portraits the mythical Dutchman (played by James Mason) paints of her imagined, then actual likeness. As such, Gardner is positioned throughout the film alongside a myriad of statues, serving to, as Susan Felleman notes, "imbue her with mythic aura" (figure 3.4).[17]

Connections to *Pandora* pervade *The Barefoot Contessa*, suggesting a conscious reflection on Gardner's image in Mankiewicz's consideration of Hollywood stardom. Pre-production letters between Allenberg and Mankiewicz indicate that James Mason had initially agreed to take on the role of the Count, only production delays on *A Star Is Born* (Mason playing a myth exposed) forcing him to drop out of the project.[18] The repeat pairing would have seen Gardner's character in both cases fall in love with a variation on a myth personified—one the doomed seafarer of a seventeenth-century

Fig. 3.4: Ava Gardner as goddess in *Pandora and the Flying Dutchman* (MGM, 1951).

narrative, and the other the princely hero of a fairy tale. In addition, British cinematographer Jack Cardiff had a key creative input into the visual imagery surrounding Gardner in both films; actor Marius Goring plays a poet who kills himself for love of Pandora, as well as the South American millionaire whose ego Maria serves; both films open in the present day followed by a flashback to a Spanish tavern; and both films cite Omar Khayyam's "The Moving Finger writes; And, having writ, Moves on."[19] The dispersion of this imagery into Gardner's off-screen life—and death—moreover creates a discourse of meta-mythology around Gardner. The knowledge that Frank Sinatra claimed *The Barefoot Contessa*'s statue of Maria, relocating it to the gardens of his Coldwater Canyon home, therefore serves as more than prurient fascination. Similarly, a statue of Gardner as Pandora commissioned after her death has since 1998 overlooked Tossa de Mar, casting the star in stone as a lasting myth at the location of her character's fictional creation.

The blurring of characterization and star text occurring here is at play beyond the specificity of these goddess parallels. The image in *The Barefoot Contessa* of Maria posing at her film's premiere to the flash of photographers' cameras, illustrating her achievement of stardom, frequently appears in documentaries without reference to the film, suggesting a seamless interchangeability between star image and fictional character. *Contessa* was central to the construction of Gardner's image as a star whose glamour belied an earthy nature and desire for an untrammeled lifestyle. Her affair with the married Sinatra and their subsequent marriage, despite the strong disapproval of MGM, to whom she was under contract, suggested a female star willing to confront Hollywood's moral hypocrisies founded on public versus private identities. *The Barefoot Contessa* commenced the development of an image of Gardner as a star more at home with the personal freedoms of Europe than as a Hollywood star in Beverly Hills. The notion that Gardner was the embodiment of Maria's search for autonomy was evident in reviews of the film, even as they simultaneously reinforced the myth of her stardom. *Harper's Bazaar*, for example, drew direct parallels with Ava's lifestyle, describing her as:

> a sloe-eyed beauty from another part of the South, who built her own legend by being fatally fascinated to a long line of movie stars, saxophone players, crooners and bullfighters. In *The Barefoot*

Contessa she is, as usual, her astonishingly lovely self in the role of a Spanish dancer, to the skilfully underplayed amazement of Humphrey Bogart, and to the delight of Mankiewicz who wrote and directed the movie.[20]

While they reference her sexual nonconformity, the remarks clearly and notably distinguish between Bogart as an actor and Gardner as a star with a "legend" drawn around her beauty and revelations about her private life. This markedly ignores the impact on Bogart's star identity of publicity surrounding his combative third marriage to Mayo Methot and the mythological bliss of his fourth marriage to Lauren Bacall. In *Colliers* magazine, a photo story including a still from the scene of Maria dancing with Spanish gypsies, representative of the character's attempts to escape her own myth, suggested her love of going barefoot meant Gardner "had the time of her life"[21] in the dance and throughout filming. Gardner herself remarked: "If *Mogambo* was the best I ever did as an actress, this was the apogee of my life as a so-called star,"[22] so defined by the film did she become. At the same time, her reference to being a "so-called star" points to a self-imaging through which Gardner attempts to distance herself from star mythology. Commenting in her autobiography on the difficulty of coping with the construction of her image by the press, Gardner relates a tale of bumping into Bette Davis at the Madrid Hilton: "I went up to her and said, 'Miss Davis, I'm Ava Gardner and I'm a great fan of yours.' And do you know, she behaved exactly as I wanted her to behave. 'Of course you are, my dear,' she said. 'Of course you are.' And she swept on. Now that's a star."[23]

While all biographical evidence suggests Gardner's nonconformist resistance to Hollywood's constraints—her conspicuous affairs and her move to Europe at the height of her stardom, for example—the idea of a reluctant or even nonexistent star identity acts as its own constructed myth. Following Gardner's arrival for filming in Rome, Mankiewicz wrote a desperate letter to Allenberg, the agent for both the director and his star, indicating his concern that the film's production would exceed its budget and financial and creative control would be assumed by United Artists due to Gardner's excessive spending. (Bogart's expenses were also mentioned as a contributing factor, but notably only in passing.) Indeed, Mankiewicz suggested: "What I write to you now is probably more urgent and more important than any communication you have received from me heretofore, in relation to our actual production." The detailed expenses outlined by Mankiewicz—which included a telephone bill for her suite at a luxury hotel, the rental of a car which sat outside the hotel while she suffered a cold, and the engagement of a secretary and five staff when the production moved her into an apartment—serve as an intervening disruption to Gardner's suppression of her own star mythology.[24]

The narrative of *The Barefoot Contessa*, furthermore, maintains its association of Greek mythology with stardom throughout the film, notably continuing as Maria discards her life as a movie star in anticipation of entering the world of European nobility as the next Countess Torlato-Favrini. The statue commissioned by her future husband represents a version of the ancestral paintings through which the family's history is explained to Maria on her arrival at the castle inhabited by the Count and his sister. It simultaneously indicates the distance through which he relates to his future wife, viewing Maria as an appropriate visual metaphor for his family's historic status, while unable to relate to her sexually due to the impotence he hides from Maria until their wedding night. The relationship has echoes in Hollywood producer Edwards' treatment of Maria as a star whose independence and lack of attraction to him must be conquered, and millionaire Bravano's purchase of her as false evidence of his machismo. When Maria's confidante Harry Dawes visits her at the Count's residence while on location and views her posing for the statue commissioned by her future husband, he suggests that if news travels to Beverly Hills, stars will be keen to convert their own likenesses into stone, reemphasizing the film's portrayal of stars as modern American versions of Europe's mythical gods (figure 3.5).

Even more consistently, however, the narrative makes self-referential reference to myth through Cinderella, the fairy-tale myth translated to the screen by Walt Disney only one year prior to *The Barefoot Contessa* and established as a stardom trope in *Ella Cinders*. Maria's penchant for going barefoot is first on display when Harry visits her in her dressing room at the Madrid club and spies her bare feet and those of a man behind a curtain. When he later visits Maria at her parents' home to discuss a screen test, she explains that hiding barefoot in the dirt as a child during the Spanish Civil War made her less afraid. The further connection made with her adult taste for meaningless sex with men deemed of a lower class is suggested

Fig. 3.5: Maria Vargas/D'Amata (Ava Gardner) embodies the modern-day myth of the movie star goddess but remains barefoot in *The Barefoot Contessa* (United Artists, 1954).

by her dressing-room encounter and explained to Harry as another version of her search for safety among the dirt. Shoes represent her fear of being bought by wealthy men and performing "in my shoes and on display for men and women to examine," something already conveyed in the Madrid club scene when we see only the reactions of the men in the audience rather than Maria's performance. The significance of shoes as a metaphor for the traps in Maria's life is clear from Mankiewicz's early script notes: "Shoes were her particular abomination. They were the symbols of restraint, demand, hateful authority and artificiality."[25]

Maria's achievement of local stardom in Madrid has provided her with little relief from fear, yet her own fandom demonstrates the potency of the Hollywood mythology that will eventually ensnare her. Stills of movie stars and directors are pinned to the walls of her dressing room, and as Maria tells Harry of her admiration of the work of Lubitsch and Fleming, she expresses her wonder at his direction of Jean Harlow and Carole Lombard.

As the conversation demonstrates the international stretch of Hollywood's mythology, it also shows Maria in its thrall, desiring a seamless passage from local to movie stardom, and pointing to the central conflict between the myth and the need for freedom that will ensure Maria's demise. A character Mankiewicz modeled on himself, Harry represents the creative arm of the business that serves to legitimize Hollywood's mythology, while set against the destructive economic power of Edwards and the cynical manipulation practiced by Muldoon. Before surrendering to Bravano's purchase of her as an "asset," as a defiant response to Edwards's attempt at control, Maria explains to Harry her unhappiness at living "half in the dirt and half out." She describes her life as a modern-day myth:

> In many ways, it's been beyond my dreams, like a fairy tale of this century, and I have been la Cenicienta [Cinderella] . . . I have gowns and jewels of silver and gold. I have a coach not pulled by four horses but with the power of two hundred. Thousands of lonely men write each month that they dream of me. Mothers give my name to their babies. And young girls rub their faces with a soap, which I am paid to say that I use but which I do not. And I have so many other things, everything in the world which can be rented.

Maria's description critiques the consumerist strategies underpinning a myth of stardom that constructs fandom yet remains fundamentally unattainable and temporary, locating star and fan within a false mythological narrative. Moreover, this twentieth-century Cinderella's fairy tale represents restriction rather than freedom, as illustrated by the shoe metaphor to which she returns: "Did it ever occur to you, Harry, that the prince looked everywhere for Cinderella just so that he could put the shoe *back* on her foot."

Harry and Maria later share their private joke when she insists on posing in bare feet for the statue the Count commissions to immortalize her in stone as a goddess. Her relationship with the Count represents an attempt to escape Hollywood, reverting to the Cinderella myth through which stardom has already failed her. Europe's castle and prince, the symbols of a more traditional fairy tale, predictably provide further entrapment, made plain by the image of Maria peering through a small square window in the ancient doors of the castle as Harry leaves the Contessa to a platonic marriage on her wedding night. When Maria reveals her attempt to provide the Count with a son and heir means she is carrying the chauffeur's child, her husband promptly shoots them both to death, again bringing this thematic concern of the stardom narrative to the fore. The statue of Maria that looms large in the castle grounds when Harry rushes to prevent his premonition of doom reconnects the myths that have proven their incompatibility with the "real" world. Yet, while the Count's heir dies with Maria, positioning this fairy tale in the past, the potency and sustainability of Hollywood's modern mythology remains. As Harry notes with blue skies returning to the site of Maria's funeral: "We'll get a good day's work done tomorrow."

Paddy Chayefsky's *The Goddess* (1958) provides an even more explicit intersection with the biopic genre. Playing out as a narrative of three acts—portraits of "a Young Girl," "a Young Woman," and "a Goddess"—the film follows Rita Shawn (née Emily Ann Faulkner), played by Kim Stanley, from an impoverished childhood in the American South to Hollywood stardom and mental illness. The narrative is clearly framed around public perceptions of Marilyn Monroe as a biographical text, and therefore includes an early local marriage, a second to a jealous Joe DiMaggio–style sports figure, the "casting couch" playing a role in her success, a peak of Hollywood stardom, and the mental illness that she learns may have been passed on to her daughter (something Monroe purportedly feared in relation to her own mother). The narrative events occur around a characterization that borrows heavily from Monroe's star image in a combination of ambition and sexuality countered by anxiety, emotional dependency, and repression. By purporting to be a fictional narrative while drawing on the biography of a star at the peak of her career in 1958, *The Goddess* represents a fairly audacious film. One critic indeed reported on a disclaimer issued by Chayefsky following protests from Monroe's third husband, playwright Arthur Miller.[26] Many reviewers were more concerned with what they viewed as Stanley's inability to convey Monroe's charisma. Philip Scheuer wrote in the *Los Angeles Times*: "Miss Stanley has not the conventional youth, beauty or glamour of the Hollywood luminary."[27] Drawing attention to Stanley's dissimilar acting background, defined by Broadway, the Method, and television plays, the critic for the *Saturday Review* suggested: "Aside from the physical miscasting, Miss Stanley is all too plainly a rather intellectualized actress making her own comment on a character she both pities and abhors." As Cohan notes, the film neglects to includes scenes in which Rita Shawn can be seen acting, something that "erases her agency as a performer"[28] and may equally have been a means of limiting the exposure of any disparities in screen presence.

In addition to the film's specific citing of Monroe's star identity, however, the narrative implicitly critiques star mythology through reference to other stardom narratives. Emily's youthful dream of being discovered like Lana Turner, for example, culminates in the now blonde Rita sitting in a Hollywood restaurant similar to the actors' hang-out depicted in *Imitation of Life* (Douglas Sirk, 1959), pointedly attired in the same halter neck-style dress later worn by Turner's character when movie stardom beckons. In addition, Rita's return to her home town for her mother's funeral is accompanied by fans and photographers who surround the house and the burial site, emphasizing connections to the fictional narratives of *What Price Hollywood?* and the *A Star Is Born* films. The limited sense of the industry and of Rita's position within it as a star and performer, however, leaves *The Goddess* with a referencing of Hollywood culture and biography surrounding rather than informing the depiction of a movie star sliding further into mental illness—the film bears little resemblance to *Sunset Boulevard*, for example. Where it conforms to the stardom narrative, however, is in its mirroring of the genre's escape theme, as the sanctuary Hollywood initially provided for Emily is repeated in the final scenes. While Rita explains to her first husband that the stardom she achieved is "a fraud"—disturbing the Lana Turner myth—her assistant and companion explains to him why they will return to Hollywood: "She'll go on making movies because that's all she knows to do. And whatever happens after that, happens."

The Hollywood Star Biopic

Narratives that explore the theme of the combination of reality, image, and myth in the stardom film provide an obvious and direct connection to the biopic. The hybrid film, which dramatizes the life and career of a Hollywood movie star, exploits some of the tropes of both genres, including the personal characteristics, talent, or skills that realize the protagonist's fame (star charisma) and the challenge to historical and community norms that their success requires (escape). The films equally exhibit fundamental contradictions as the genres collide. Dennis Bingham asserts that "the aim of all biopics [is] to reveal the 'real person' behind the public persona,"[29] while the central theme of the fictional stardom narrative is to construct and maintain the star myth. This core clash between the mythology of the stardom genre and the intended truth of the biopic, which further connects the latter to the historical film (even as this veracity becomes a matter of contention), establishes an additional narrative approach to stardom mythology. Ideas of performance and star imagery inherent in narratives about movie stars, moreover, necessarily complicate any purported aim to bring the "real person" to the screen in films that are, after all, still fictional narratives.

Jean-Louis Comolli's contention that the biopic's depiction of an historical figure by an actor provides "one body too much" competing for the audience's belief[30] becomes complicated still further when both bodies are those of movie stars, bringing the additional star image of the character into play alongside the "real person" and the image of the star playing him or her. Industry and cultural context simultaneously form a backdrop to the treatment of both individual stars and star mythology. George Custen traces the path of the biopic from the prestige film of the early studio era depicting the historical significance of scientists and politicians to a shift that occurred during the 1950s. In the postwar era, the declining impact of the Production Code and its attempt at the moral guardianship of the nation made way for films that would dramatize the colorful lives of movie stars more realistically than the periodic examples from earlier decades had been able to achieve. At the same time, the diminishing power of the studios following the Paramount Decision, alongside an audience shift to the suburbs and television, made space for independent producers less daunted to confront the star myth created by the studio system.[31]

While the biopics of the 1950s began to dramatize aspects of movie stars' lives formerly hidden or disguised in entertainment biopics—for example, the homosexuality of star songwriters Cole Porter and Lorenz Hart playing out as marriage problems or unrequited love and alcoholism in *Night and Day* (Michael Curtiz, 1946) and *Words and Music* (Norman Taurog, 1948), respectively—by increasingly delving into drama-filled areas of their private lives, the films often, conversely, seem more akin to fictional but veiled narratives, such as *The Goddess*, than to a biographical journey through a star's career. James Cagney's performance as Lon

Chaney in *Man of a Thousand Faces* (Joseph Pevney, 1957), for example, centers on the impact his ex-wife's (played by Dorothy Malone) mental illness has on family life with his son and new wife (played by Jane Greer), while in *Valentino* (Lewis Allen, 1951) the star's (played by Anthony Dexter) career is drawn through a narrative focusing on a doomed, illicit love affair. Both films refer to the mythology of movie stardom historically articulated through the fictional narratives of the stardom film genre. For Chaney, Hollywood provides an escape from the negative associations of the theatre where his ex-wife attempted suicide on stage, and the opportunity to develop a relatable screen identity as an outsider through a visual disguise. Similarly, *Valentino* touches on the female audience's response to the star, signifying the importance of fandom to the star system. Yet, within both films these narrative themes customarily explored through the lens of star mythology take a back seat to the introduction of more culturally controversial topics aimed at representing the "real" and personal lives of these stars.

The surfeit of movie star biopics appearing in the following decades, however, points to ways in which the mythology of the stardom narrative becomes incorporated into the biopic, as well as how attempts are made to disturb both generic approaches and their attendant myths. The breakdown in the studio system and increasing space for independent production that occurred through the postwar era becomes a crucial element in this shift, illustrated in the unusual circumstance of the production of two biopics centered on the life story of Jean Harlow and released in 1965. Both films were prompted by the publication of Irving Shulman's salacious book *Harlow: An Intimate Biography* in 1964, produced side by side and released within months of each other the following year. Such parallel production of the same subject matter was unprecedented and signaled a new and not wholly welcome era of filmmaking. *Life* magazine text for an article ultimately published in an alternative version suggested the occurrence was "a manifestation of the new anarchistic ere [*sic*] in Hollywood. Traditionally, no respectable film company would film another's story, let alone use its title."[32]

The resulting antagonism between the two independent newcomers garnered much of the press attention around the films, and followed a period of production during which Joseph E. Levine, at least, attempted to avoid the trap of exploiting the context of a Production Code in its dying months and ending up with a tabloid-style film.[33] Levine's Embassy Pictures was a company focused on exhibition and distribution before Levine produced his first Hollywood saga in 1964, *The Carpetbaggers* (Edward Dmytryk), which starred Carroll Baker as a tragic movie star who dies in a drunken car crash. Levine would go on to produce a further Hollywood narrative, *The Oscar*, in 1966, which led Philip K. Scheuer of the *Los Angeles Times* to complain that Levine was "on that anti-Hollywood kick again."[34] His *Harlow* biopic produced with Paramount starred Baker in a plush Technicolor production directed by Gordon Douglas, with a supporting cast of respected co-stars that included Martin Balsam and Angela Lansbury. The second film (although the first to be released) was produced by Bill Sargent, an entrepreneur whose only experience of film production was the filming of Richard Burton in *Hamlet* on Broadway for screening in theatres, a method of production *Life* reported he had planned to exploit again for the film.[35] His version of *Harlow* was a less costly black and white biopic starring Carol Lynley among a similar roster of famous names including Ginger Rogers and Barry Sullivan, and directed by Alex Segal whose experience had been gained largely in television. The antagonism between the two directors was played out in the press, again emphasizing the unconventional post-studio system context of the productions. As the owner of the screen rights to Shulman's book, Levine positioned Sargent as an industry interloper, describing him as "a leech" whose behavior was "against the ethics and the code of the industry." Sargent, meanwhile, adopted outrageous publicity stunts that included flying a blimp over the 1965 Academy Awards ceremony inviting the television audience to "See Sargent's *Harlow* starring Carol Lynley."[36]

Neither film was critically well received, and in both cases much of the commentary circulated around how successfully each achieved authentic depictions of 1930s Hollywood and the star identity of Harlow. Levine's purchase of the screen rights to Shulman's book lent his film a certain legitimacy in terms of Harlow's life story. On the other hand, the book itself had created quite a furor amongst Hollywood insiders close to Harlow who disputed many of the claims that were subsequently repeated in the film. The narratives of both films, moreover, used extensive poetic license in depicting Harlow's story, both choosing to omit her childhood and include composite characters. Levine's version in addition creates fictional names for MGM and Louis B. Mayer and fails to include what most biographies have depicted as Harlow's contented relationship with movie star William Powell, something that in Sargent's film provides a counter to more sexualized imagery and a melodramatic narrative (even as, again, the character has a loose basis and alternative name). Steven Cohan, in fact, argues both biopics more determinedly draw on what he terms the "bio-persona" of Marilyn Monroe than that of Harlow in their depiction of a character who conveys sensuality disguising her apparent frigidity, and studies acting in New York in order to be taken seriously.[37]

When the second *Harlow* starring Baker was released six weeks after Sargent's rushed version appeared, attention was drawn, however, to the budget and expertise on display in this visibly superior production and its consequent ability to depict an air of Hollywood glamour appropriate to the narrative. *Life*'s description of Levine's film as the "$4 million deluxe version" in comparison to Sargent's "quickie, made in just eight days in a new process called Electronovision"[38] set the background for a press conversation illustrating a nostalgia for the kind of glamour Harlow's star text represented. Much of this discussion revolved around the Baker-led film due to both its higher production values and costumes designed by legendary Hollywood costumier Edith Head. In an article in the trade magazine *Western Apparel Industry*, the author praised the film's evocation of the "contrived, deliberate glamour" of Hollywood's past, as Head associated her designs with a return to a more feminine look: "Style-wise we have been drifting for several seasons toward the look of the Thirties, and I think 'Harlow' will have an impact to solidify the trend and make girls look like girls and not like tomboys."[39] *Daily Variety* similarly drew attention to the combination of set design and costume that distinguished the film from its rival: "It is a return to glamour in picture-making, lusciously caught in Panavision and Technicolor, with sets costing a fortune and costumes by Edith Head seldom duplicated in recent years" (figure 3.6).[40]

Mirroring the reception of *The Goddess*, however, the stars of both films were critiqued for their inability to convey Harlow's screen charisma. The *New York Times* took aim at the first release with "front, center and anything but alluring, Carol Lynley as the nation's movie sex goddess of the thirties. She squeaks, occasionally furrows her youthful brow and twitches her nostrils."[41] The *Chicago Tribune* wrote of Carroll Baker's performance: "Despite elaborate efforts at makeup and a $100,000 Edith Head wardrobe, she seems to suggest a no-longer-girlish suburban housewife hurrying to a slightly

Fig. 3.6: Joseph Levine's *Harlow* (Paramount, 1965) surpasses its competitor in glamour, while the stars of both films suffer comparisons with their star character.

distasteful evening of bridge . . . Harlow is the one people will come to see; she doesn't even come into sight."[42] The original casting of Judy Garland as Harlow's mother alongside Lynley—Garland was recast after one day on set when she subsequently failed to attend and was replaced by Ginger Rogers—reemphasizes the attempt of both productions to find ways to draw on both a glamorous Hollywood past and the evocation of stardom, Garland as a specific reference point for the history of the stardom narrative. The Levine film illustrates this most notably by repeating some visual and narrative tropes of the genre's films. The film introduces its protagonist, for example, by following her as one of the mass of extras and bit-part players entering a studio and passing through costume and make-up onto the back lot. We subsequently view her journey from extra to star through silent cinema bathing and custard pie scenes, clothes fittings, and make-up to construct her image, and the studio's management of her assortment of fan mail. A salient scene in which a young blonde woman styled after her idol boards a bus on which posters of Harlow on the cover of *Photoplay* adorn the walls similarly points to both the indicators of success and the significance of fandom repeatedly depicted as core elements of the stardom story. Harlow's narrative in the biopic therefore becomes a realization of the mythology of the stardom narrative's fictional counterparts, even as its biographical authenticity is hotly contested.

Movement Between Screen Media

The resurgence in the star biopic that occurred in the 1970s and 1980s spoke to a nostalgia for the glamour evoked by Hollywood movie stars of the studio era that was similarly evident in blockbuster disaster movies including *The Towering Inferno* (John Guillermin, 1974) with stars William Holden, Fred Astaire, and Jennifer Jones, *Earthquake* (Mark Robson, 1974) starring Charlton Heston and Ava Gardner, and *Airport* (George Seaton, 1970) with Burt Lancaster, Dean Martin, and Van Heflin. The charismatic value of the movie star as stardom's heightened form persisted, reinforced by reruns of classic films on American television and prompting both nostalgia and fascination for a Hollywood era that at this stage seemed long passed. At the same time, with biopics no longer viewed as prestige pictures or as box-office winners, the subsequent movement of the movie star biopic into television enabled an association with Hollywood glamour the medium otherwise lacked. As Cohan notes, the shift of the stardom narrative into both the biopic and television during the 1970s and 1980s was a product of the Hollywood studios' increasing concentration on male stars, male audiences, and the male writers, directors and producers who drove the majority of films.[43]

Drawing on the dominance of female star narratives in the stardom film, the television biopic has repeatedly turned to stars such as Marilyn Monroe, Elizabeth Taylor, and Judy Garland to both articulate the mythology of Hollywood stardom and expose the damaging effects of its patriarchal culture, tailoring the films' approaches to these individual star images. Cohan highlights the narrative construction of Monroe's life and career as an amalgamation of information gleaned from various biographies and documentaries, an "imitation of life," in Custen's terms.[44] From the 1974 ABC television movie *The Sex Symbol*, which took its cue from *The Goddess* by dramatizing Monroe's life through a "fictional" character, to *The Secret Life of Marilyn Monroe* miniseries on Lifetime in 2015, and a

Netflix biopic entitled *Blonde* in development as an adaptation of the Joyce Carol Oates novel, Monroe has been the subject of multiple dramatizations on television, as well as on film. Drawing on Sarah Churchwell's identification of an essential "uncertainty" in the Monroe story relayed through the reinforcement of an assumed history in written biographies, Cohan suggests a similarly incoherent fusion of the factual and the fictional in the screen construction of the "Monroe bio-persona,"[45] one that ultimately generates an identity of Monroe as a movie star robbed of her agency by a variety of male figures and power structures that are personal, industrial, and political.[46]

Various television biopics of Elizabeth Taylor have focused perhaps even more centrally on the drama of her personal life, often refracting this through an identity as a movie star as opposed to an actress. While NBC's 1995 miniseries *Liz: The Elizabeth Taylor Story*, starring Sherilyn Fenn, covered Taylor's narrative from childhood through to her campaigning for AIDS awareness, two more recent screen narratives notably focused on Taylor's relationship with actor Richard Burton, both drawing attention to her embodiment of classic Hollywood stardom in contrast to the persistence of Burton's highbrow stage identity. Critical responses to Lifetime's *Liz & Dick* (2012), which starred Lindsay Lohan, and the BBC's *Burton and Taylor* (2013) also traded in cultural hierarchies—even as they reclaimed Taylor's acting credentials—as well as returning to the genre's core problematic dynamic of the portrayal of a movie star by an actor less associated with movie stardom. As respected actors in a BBC production, Helena Bonham Carter and Dominic West were, for example, hailed as "excellent" by the *Guardian*'s reviewer, with the understanding that "It's an almost impossible task, for two actors to act perhaps the greatest ever acting double act."[47] In a roasting of *Liz & Dick*, moreover, the *Hollywood Reporter* labeled Lohan "woeful as Taylor from start to finish," suggesting the actress was so obviously ill equipped for the role that the casting was a ploy to ensure high ratings for "an instant classic of unintentional hilarity."[48]

While the shift of the biopic to television has been extensive in recent decades, the Hollywood biopic has provided a space for individual critiques of the industry and its treatment of female stars alongside small screen versions of the genre. Such contextualization of the female star narrative is evident in Levine's independent production of *Harlow* starring Carroll Baker, which depicted sexual abuse as a commonplace approach to female stardom in the male-dominated studio system. The 1982 biopic *Frances* (Graeme Clifford) starring Jessica Lange similarly disturbs the mythologizing of stardom through the story of Paramount star Frances Farmer, representing stardom as less American Dream than nightmare (a television version starring Susan Blakely followed soon after in 1983). Frances is introduced as a high school student with an independent streak, winning an essay prize in which she questions God's existence. By the time she takes a sponsored trip to Russia as a roundabout means of hitting New York as a budding actress and ultimately winds up at Paramount Studios, the film has already disrupted the stardom narrative's trope of escape, setting up Broadway as an escape route from moral probity and Hollywood as an unhappy and unsatisfying replacement.

While the film associates itself with the stardom genre again in scenes such as when Frances surreptitiously observes the head of the studio (played by Allan Rich) viewing her first performance, the narrative makes plain both the studio system within which her career functions, and her unwillingness to submit to its control. The film steers away, however, from providing a stereotypical contrast with an East Coast stage nirvana, showing Frances attempting a Broadway career by starring in *Golden Boy* to escape Hollywood control, but being exploited for her box-office appeal before being replaced by a "real" actress for the West End run, as well as being emotionally discarded by playwright Clifford Odets on his wife's return home. Therefore, the label of mental illness attached to Frances, which sees her imprisoned, institutionalized, abused, and lobotomized, the narrative suggests, is facilitated by a culture in which the star's resistance to conformity and control is deemed evidence of a disturbed mind. At the same time, the mythology of stardom, to which Frances's mother Lillian (played by the star of *The Goddess*, Kim Stanley) is in thrall, acts as the catalyst for others to define Frances as the crazed movie star of the headlines. While Frances is in recovery, Lillian writes fake fan letters and brings the press to town to force her daughter back into the movies and into a life she herself once desired. Her belief in the mythology of stardom drives her attempts to control Frances: "You had it all—beauty, a brilliant career, a wonderful husband. You are a movie star. You're just going to throw it away, huh? Throw it away and become a nobody. Have you any idea what it's like to be a nobody?"

The authorities simultaneously collude with the press in front page depictions of mental instability, and local servicemen pay off hospital staff to allow them to rape a movie star. When Frances realizes her mother would continue returning her to institutions where she is regarded as mentally ill with the aim of ultimately confining her to a star identity, the film's destruction of the stardom myth is complete, except for a final coda. Having found faith and transformed into a sedate version of her former self, she appears on the NBC television show *This Is Your Life* in 1958 and describes her aims to help those who have had similar experiences and to reflect upon why others had sought to erroneously label her as mentally ill. Host Ralph Edwards (played by Donald Craig) reveals the show has facilitated some offers from the Hollywood studios, as Frances is presented with a car to assist her in her renewed career and thrown an after-show party at the Hollywood Roosevelt. Before the credits roll, we learn that Frances Farmer made one additional film (*The Party Crashers* [Bernard Girard, 1958]) before moving to Indianapolis and becoming the host of a daytime television show; in *Frances Farmer Presents*, which ran for five years from 1958, she introduced movies, discussed their stars, and interviewed celebrities. Perhaps the most destructive quality of the star myth, the film suggests, is that stardom in all its forms becomes a place from which you can check out but never leave.

Judy Garland as Biopic Subject

Judy Garland's appearances as the subject of biopic exploration can be understood as part of the shift from film to television and back again, drawing on an identity constructed through multiple written biographies. The Garland bio-persona intervenes explicitly in stardom mythology as articulated through fictional stardom narratives, including implicit self-reflection on her own, positioning Garland's narrative in the context of the construction and destruction of the myth. Moreover, Garland's identity as biopic subject functions specifically in relation to the impact of the Hollywood star system on both personal life and performance, blurring the on- and off-screen worlds as the context for the bio-persona develops across the various biopics. NBC's 1978 television movie *Rainbow* (directed by fellow MGM child star Jackie Cooper) limits itself to the early movie career of Garland (played by Andrea McArdle), confronting—if timidly—the pressures placed on the young performer by MGM's star system. Focusing on Garland's vaudeville beginnings through to her recording of "Over the

Rainbow," the film suggests an ambitious talent succumbing to the demands—drugs and diets—of an uncaring system represented by Louis B. Mayer (played by Martin Balsam). Garland's only relief comes through her necessary dependence upon the protection of individuals like Roger Edens (played by Michael Parks), her father Frank (played by Don Murray) and, at times, her mother Ethel (played by Piper Laurie), the latter presented more favorably in this narrative than in others or, indeed, than Garland herself depicted her mother in interviews.[49]

The 2001 miniseries *Life with Judy Garland: Me and My Shadows*, which aired on ABC and was adapted from daughter Lorna Luft's *Me and My Shadows: A Family Memoir*,[50] stars Judy Davis alongside Carley Alves and Tammy Blanchard as younger Garlands. Covering the star's career from child star to her death, the biopic suggests an adult Garland fully aware of her star identity and constantly disturbing the boundaries between her real and fictional worlds. When she threatens to jump from a hotel room in order to avoid the bill, for example, she asks the manager, "How's it gonna look for you when Dorothy jumps out your window?" Garland calms her young daughter with the assurance, "Don't be silly, sweetheart, it's all part of the myth." When MGM sends her to see a psychiatrist during the filming of *The Pirate* (Vincente Minnelli, 1948) due to her erratic behavior and continued drug use, she asks the analyst which "Judy Garland" he would prefer to discuss. Offering various alternatives constructed through *Photoplay* and *Life* magazine, she describes Frances Gumm as "long gone . . . too fat, she had a funny name, she was so boring we had to get rid of her." The characterization of Garland's knowing separation of a real identity as Frances and a constructed one as Judy is clearly aimed at, on the one hand, suggesting the emotional instability delineated through the narrative. The scene simultaneously points to the essential myth of stardom as a combination of the "real" person and glamorous star, the ordinary and extraordinary mixture upon which the construction of stardom is based. The narrative confrontation of the studio's vision of an undesirable reality necessarily extinguished and a constructed star image (including a constructed "real" persona), then, works to expose the mythological construction of stardom ultimately largely upheld in films within the stardom genre.

At the same time, Garland's charismatic value is repeatedly reinforced through the miniseries, for example, with the depiction of her legendary

1951 opening at the Palace Theatre in New York. Using Garland's original recordings and representing the performance with overlapping images of an enraptured audience of celebrated stars, the sequence presents Garland's stage presence as evidence of the star quality challenged by MGM's decision to release her the previous year. Her performance of "Over the Rainbow" seated at the edge of the stage and dressed as the tramp of "A Couple of Swells" in *Easter Parade* (Charles Walters, 1948) simultaneously references *A Star Is Born*'s "Born in a Trunk" sequence. The latter film takes a prominent position in the biopic's dramatization of Garland's narrative, with scenes depicting the filming of "The Man That Got Away" and the film's premiere intercut with newsreel footage, again acting to reemphasize Garland's charismatic value as a star and performer. Jack Warner's appearance as an observer on set and in the screening room as he insists on a production schedule and cuts to the edited film is, moreover, set against this star identity, reinforcing a dynamic of creative star versus financially driven studio. Warner's shifting of the blame for editing decisions onto "orders from New York" additionally parallels *A Star Is Born* and Oliver Niles's explanation for having to release Norman Maine from his contract. This overlapping of *A Star Is Born*'s stardom narrative, its referencing of Garland's mythical star identity, and this bio-persona and its paralleling with the character of Maine also potently occurs in a scene depicting the filming of Esther's dressing room conversation with Oliver Niles on the set of "Lose That Long Face." Just as *A Star Is Born* infers a relationship between the self-destructive Norman Maine that Esther describes and Garland's life experience, the scene here indicates husband and producer Sid Luft's (played by Victor Garber) realization of this correlation, as well as his own relationship to Esther's resentment, as he watches Garland's performance.

Garland's bio-persona has been revisited and recontextualized more recently in a film biopic released amidst a series of big screen musicals about singers, most notably *Bohemian Rhapsody* (Brian Singer, 2018) centered on Queen front man Freddie Mercury and the Elton John life story in *Rocketman* (Dexter Fletcher, 2019), which in turn sat alongside the release of the fourth *A Star Is Born* film. Like *Life with Judy Garland*, the 2019 release *Judy* (Rupert Goold) starring Renée Zellweger draws on the mythology that moves between Garland's stage and screen identity(ies), fictional stardom narratives, and biopics, while signaling more explicitly the gendered aspects of Garland's experience for a contemporary audience living in a climate of exposure of abusive practices in the media world. Critical responses to the film had precedent in earlier fictional stardom narratives and biopics in their treatment of the relationship between star performer and star character. Oscar buzz around Zellweger's performance as a triumphant comeback after an acting hiatus resonated with the hysteria around Garland's return to the screen in *A Star Is Born* and the one-woman show that made her loss to Grace Kelly on Academy Awards night so unexpected. (In a telegram to Garland, Groucho Marx called it "the biggest robbery since Brink's.") *Variety* suggested that:

> Even around the time she was hoofing to Oscar-nominated effect in "Chicago"—and sure enough, you can draw a jagged line from the stage-hungry striver Zellweger played there to her spotlight-trained, love-starved Garland—it would have been near-impossible to imagine the actress in this role. Nearly two decades later, the casting makes bittersweet sense: A onetime American sweetheart who relinquished the burdensome title, she plays Garland, with palpable affection and feeling, as one who's been over the rainbow and back again.[51]

Depicting Zellweger's choice to step away from the movie star spotlight for six years as something akin to the highs and lows of Garland's life, the author attempts to draw parallels that bear little fruit but were frequently repeated on release of the film. So essentialist is the connection between the subject and performer of the stardom narrative at this stage assumed to be, that such links are necessarily drawn. Zellweger's speech on winning the Academy Award, during which the actress noted, "Judy Garland did not receive this honor in her time," recalls again the unfulfilled symbolic climax of her subject's comeback tale that contrasts with her own.

Judy focuses on the final months of Garland's life spent in London as she performed at the Talk of the Town nightclub. Early scenes show Garland in financial despair when she returns to the Los Angeles hotel where she has been living with children Lorna and Joey to find their room has been released and belongings put in storage due to her unpaid bills. In contrast with *Life with Judy Garland*, which transforms this scenario into a game in which the family wear their wardrobes out of the hotel to avoid payment, Garland here is left homeless and at the mercy of ex-husband Sidney Luft's attempts to gain custody of the children. Her trip to London therefore sees Garland in search of the economic power required to maintain a family life, even as she must leave her children behind to do so.

The film uses a series of flashbacks to connect Garland as a child performer to the child-like, middle-aged star who has to be literally pushed onto the stage by her English charge Rosalyn (played by Jessie Buckley) on opening night, and whose shows are plagued by her unreliability, which eventually leads to her being replaced by British skiffle favorite Lonnie Donegan (played by John Dalgleish). Early scenes on the set of *The Wizard of Oz* (Victor Fleming, 1939), therefore, both serve as explicit reminders of the young Garland and the character of Dorothy upon which her star image is constructed—as Garland suggests in *Life with Judy Garland*—and point to *Judy*'s running theme of the star's desire to find, more than return to, her home. These scenes additionally repeat the conventional narrative of Garland's stardom as a cautionary tale of the commodification of stardom by the studio system, as the pill consumption established through a business rationale of the construction of a star image recurs throughout the film and signals Garland's lack of physical and emotional well-being.

Variety suggests that the film "recontextualizes Garland's story for a post #MeToo audience mindful of women abused and disempowered by the industry,"[52] and this is evident in possibly the biopic genre's darkest portrayal of Louis B. Mayer. His exploitation of the myth of stardom to counter the young actress's desire for normality is revealed as self-serving by his anger at the delays she causes to production, as well as the unhappiness of her life as a star. When Mayer makes his point that Judy sings from the heart by prodding her chest, the film also directs us to the abuse Garland later suggested was part of her experience at MGM.[53] Flashback scenes that show Garland with her frequent co-star Mickey Rooney additionally highlight a distinction between the treatment of male and female stars. Rooney's seemingly carefree existence that includes the ability to partake of a hamburger at lunch, for example, is contrasted with strict studio controls on Garland's food intake, something which resonates into adulthood when we watch her lingering anxiously over a piece of cake. The film similarly suggests exploitation of Garland's stardom by the men who traverse her personal and professional lives. Manager and coproducer Luft is accused by Garland of gambling away her earnings. Soon-to-be fifth husband Mickey Deans, in turn, visits

Garland unexpectedly in London promising a lucrative deal to name a chain of U.S. movie theatres after the star. The deal, which fails to materialize, is depicted as further humiliation for a star of Garland's stature, and a further moneymaking scheme that would see her opening America's theatres rather than performing on their screens.

Alongside its thematic referencing of *The Wizard of Oz*, *Judy* draws most explicitly on *I Could Go on Singing* (Ronald Neame, 1963) and, in turn, *A Star Is Born*. In this 1963 musical drama, Garland plays singer and beloved stage performer Jenny Bowman (again drawing on her star text) visiting London to play a series of concerts at the Palladium. While in town she endeavors to establish a relationship with the unsuspecting son she gave up to an ex-partner, a widowed surgeon played by Dirk Bogarde. Garland's character is drawn in ways similar to her persona in *Judy* as a child-like star reliant on assistants and managers to maintain her professional and personal lives and ensure she reaches the stage to perform. The earlier film is additionally explicitly referenced in three specific scenes, beginning with Zellweger's first number on the Talk of the Town stage, "By Myself," which Garland also performs as Bowman at the London Palladium. Two additional scenes become contrasts in the characterization of Bowman (as a close approximation of Garland) and Garland, and in the depiction of the Garland star mythology. When Garland visits a doctor to check her vocal cords and the perceptive doctor asks whether she takes any medication for depression, her evasive quip "Four husbands" points to the denial bound up in Garland's survivor myth. In contrast, when Bowman ends up in a hospital emergency ward after overindulgence leaves her with a damaged ankle, the attempts by Bogarde's character to convince Bowman to return to the theatre for her performance are defied by the singer, who protests, "It's just not worth all the deaths that I have to die" and confesses "I've hung on to every bit of rubbish there is to hang onto in life, and I've thrown all the good bits away" (figure 3.7). The admission of personal psychological turmoil and its links to the emotional toll of performance expressed through another thinly veiled characterization of Garland (additionally drawing on *A Star Is Born*'s Esther/Oliver "Lose That Long Face" scene) suggests the ability of character and star to confront and express such vulnerabilities, which the later film challenges.

Finally, we see a reprise of a scene in *I Could Go on Singing*, in which Bowman returns late to her waiting theatre audience and swiftly calms any

Fig. 3.7: Judy Garland's depiction of an emotionally fragile star in *I Could Go on Singing* (United Artists, 1963) acts alongside *A Star Is Born* (Warner Bros., 1954) as a consistent reference point for *Judy* (Pathé, 2019).

mild annoyance and slow handclapping with joking banter. The audience backlash depicted in *Judy*, however, which extends as far as heckling and food being thrown at the star, is resolved in a later scene drawing explicitly on the Garland myth. When Garland borrows the stage from her replacement Donegan for a performance of "Over the Rainbow," Garland's potent relationship with her audience as a performer is enlisted to recuperate her stardom—and repair the temporary rupture in the star-audience relationship—through a bond with a gay male couple established earlier in the film. A scene in which Garland spends a lonely evening having dinner with the fans in their apartment points to the mutual sense of isolation connecting Garland with gay fandom that forms an essential aspect of Garland mythology. These fans take the lead, therefore, in retrieving Garland's power as a performer and consequently her stardom by initiating audience participation in the number to assist Garland in her failing performance. With the star seated at the edge of the stage in a moment reminiscent of both "Born in a Trunk" and multiple performances of "Over the Rainbow" onstage and on her CBS television show (1963–64), the scene remythologizes Garland, placing front and center the restoration of the star-audience relationship and a star image bound up in the myth of suffering and the ability to endure (figure 3.8).

The stardom film illuminates the fundamental slippage between fact and fiction central to star mythology. The blurred borders between the

Fig. 3.8: Renée Zellweger channels Judy Garland's stage and screen performances of "Over the Rainbow" as her character retrieves the star–audience relationship. *Judy* (Pathé, 2019).

myth of stardom and the authenticity promoted as part of star texts find their optimum space in narratives that at their edges flow from the depiction of fictional characters to familiar stars as the subjects of biopics, carrying the impact of star images with them. The unstable association with realness that these narratives create functions to emphasize the dominance of mythology, as characters become consumed by it, and the star myth withstands critique. The desire of stars, industry, and audience for mythology in whatever form, these films suggest, ultimately ensures the lasting relevance and appeal of Hollywood's star myth.

AFTERWORD

The preceding chapters demonstrate the stardom film genre's central imperative to maintain the myth of stardom. As narratives dramatize characters' assorted star experiences, and as films illustrate the indistinct boundaries separating reality, image, and myth, the genre suggests that stardom has the propensity for nightmare as much as for fantasy. The critiques of stardom and of the Hollywood system in its various forms that arise, however, function as fleeting disturbances to a myth of stardom that persists, and whose appeal ensures its emergence from these films intact.

While the depiction of male stardom is the focus of a number of films within the genre, and additional examples can be found beyond those explored here, the star myth undoubtedly plays out in dominant fashion through female stardom. The representation of Hollywood and stardom in early narratives as a mythological place and state through which modernity, success and self-determination might be found establishes the genre's depiction of stardom as both feminine and disruptive and binds its mythology to the broader female cultural experience. The characterization of the lives of fictional and nonfictional stars, therefore, revolves around escape, self-sacrifice, ambition, performance, conformity, and loss, alongside the achievement, satisfaction, independence, and success that serve as proof of stardom's ultimate worth.

The genre's core element of disruption is reinforced by the reemergence of stardom narratives in the second decade of the twenty-first century as they traverse the new industrial context of screen-crossing between Hollywood film, cable television, and streaming services. The shifting American cultural climate through which gender, sexual, and racial inequalities and abuse are being addressed via social movements such as #MeToo, Time's Up, and Black Lives Matter has additionally formed a backdrop to contemporary versions of the genre. While *La La Land* draws on the stardom genre to disturb the form of the musical through an updated narrative resolution acknowledging the enduring problematic for women of successfully negotiating personal and professional lives, further developments of the stardom narrative seem designed to more explicitly address cultural issues through a new lens, in particular via the star biopic. The 2019 biopic *Seberg* (Benedict Andrews), therefore, confronts the dual patriarchal controls of Hollywood and the FBI to which Jean Seberg is subjected, as the star's moral character, personal life, and patriotism are attacked due to her involvement with the racial politics of the late 1960s. Similarly, the big screen adaptation of Joyce Carol Oates's fictionalized story of Marilyn Monroe, *Blonde*, due for release in 2021 (following a 2001 miniseries version), and the currently untitled Apple TV miniseries centering on the life of Hedy Lamarr that follows the 2017 documentary *Bombshell: The Hedy Lamarr Story* (Alexandra Dean) are both expected to deliver interpretations of the stories of these stars that both celebrate their significance in Hollywood and beyond and address the climates in which their achievements occurred.

While the stardom genre's focus on female stardom has enabled the culturally disruptive representation that continues through contemporary film and television, it fails to obscure the whiteness of the stardom narrative that mirrors the racially defined manner in which Hollywood stardom has historically been constructed. During the studio era, the star system functioned overwhelmingly to deliver and feature white stars, and both fiction and nonfiction stardom narratives have been similarly racially exclusive. In the 1987 film *Hollywood Shuffle* (Robert Townsend), an aspiring African American actor resistant to stereotypical roles can become the Oscar-winning lead of a black-and-white classic or the eponymous star of *King Lear*, *Superman*, or *Rambo* only in his dreams, and therefore ultimately retreats, resigned to the impossibility of movie stardom. The deficit of films centering on African American stardom has similarly suggested race to be a barrier to stardom both in the movie business itself and in the imaginary world of the stardom narrative.

Just as television provided a home for the stardom film in the 1970s and 1980s when Hollywood temporarily stepped away from the genre, cable television in the 1980s forged a path for the development of stardom narratives that disturb the genre's racial exclusivity. In his discussion of Spike Lee's 1992 film *Malcolm X*, Thomas Doherty described the biopic as "the motion picture equivalent of an all-white neighborhood."[1] Yet, for the stardom film genre, the star biopic has proven the most accessible of hybrids in which to draw alternative racial identities into the mythology of Hollywood stardom. In some cases, this occurred through a repetition of the thinly veiled biopic that occurs through the history of stardom narratives, evidenced in films including *The Goddess* and *The Barefoot Contessa*. The 1987 miniseries *Queenie*, for example, based on the book by Michael Korda—nephew of writer, director, and producer Alexander Korda—loosely dramatizes the story of Merle Oberon, who similarly found movie stardom after leaving India. Oberon's marriage to the film impresario and her association with the nickname "Queenie" provide further basis for the diagnosis of the script as a version of her life. The character's life as depicted and played by Mia Sara draws on several stardom narrative tropes—stardom as an escape (from sexual abuse and a caste system in India), Hollywood movie stars as inspiration (Greta Garbo in George Cukor's *Camille*), and charisma as evidence of movie stardom. (When Kirk Douglas's producer-director views her screen test, he declares, "That one's a star.") The narrative's central drama, however, revolves around Queenie's suppression of her part-Indian, part-Irish identity as she "passes" as white, both as a child and as a movie star, until finally revealing at a film premiere that the Indian woman posing as her maid is her mother.

The show's casting of white actors Claire Bloom and Leigh Lawson in dark make-up to play leading roles, however, makes this a curiously dated representation of inbetween-ness in the late 1980s, as well as pointing to the future significance of cable and streaming services in representing racial diversity in the genre. The Amazon Studios backstudio series *The Last Tycoon* (2016–2017), loosely based on the F. Scott Fitzgerald novel, indeed seemed engaged in redressing some of the problematic elements of *Queenie*. The character drawn around Oberon's story and played by Jennifer Beals, for example, exploits her star power to retaliate against the sexual abuse to which she has been subjected. Similarly, the show explicitly depicts both how the exposure of the fact that the star's black maid (played by African American actress L. Scott Caldwell) is her mother would fatally damage her career, and the studio's exploitation of such an understanding to maintain control of their star.

While *The Last Tycoon* takes the broader Hollywood film industry as its focus as it serves as a recent example of disturbance of the unspoken whiteness of films about the American movie business, its maintenance of Hollywood mythology as it does so is a pertinent reminder that disruption rather than erasure of the myth is both the aim and result of most stardom narratives. Prior to streaming services, the opportunities opened up for black stories on cable television was part of its strategy to differentiate itself from the traditional networks by providing more diverse programming that emphasized cable as a new and groundbreaking form of television.[2] HBO and Showtime were key players in this approach, with TV movies such as *Introducing Dorothy Dandridge* (Martha Coolidge, 1999) and *10,000 Black Men Named George* (a 2002 film directed by Robert Townsend about the unionization of black railway porters) suggesting alternative content and quality founded in, as Jennifer Fuller explains, "historical content or gritty social realism, high production values and respected actors with significant crossover appeal."[3] Within the stardom genre, this notably occurred often through musical stars, pointing to the significance of the musical genre in providing a space for black performance less readily available in other genres of Hollywood film. Showtime's 2001 biopic *Bojangles*, starring Gregory Hines as legendary tap dancer Bill "Bojangles" Robinson, frames its story with newsreel footage of the star's funeral and of his signature stair dance, both emphasizing and authenticating Robinson's significance as an African American artist and star in the racialized context of the stardom genre. As it delineates the flaws in Robinson's character while displaying the talent and charisma that projected him to movie stardom, the narrative centers on Hollywood's confinement of Robinson to a limiting screen identity. Unsuccessful battles with Fox mogul Darryl Zanuck for more progressive roles, criticism from a black rights organization (obliquely referencing the NAACP's critiques of African American stars), and insults for the aging Robinson from radical black activists point to essential aspects of Robinson's experience of stardom that are wholly racialized and distinct from other dramatized narratives of (white) stardom.

Shonda Rhimes's screenplay for HBO's *Introducing Dorothy Dandridge* similarly sets its narrative within an authenticating framing device, with a flashback structure enabling Dandridge's telephone reminiscences with longtime friend and ex-sister-in-law Geri (ex-wife of dance star Fayard Nicholas, played by Tamara Taylor) to provide the star's perspective on events. At the same time, this flashback device both positions the film alongside stardom narratives such as *Sunset Boulevard* and *The Barefoot Contessa* and suggests the kind of ill-fated conclusion depicted through this familiar framing. While performance again becomes a marker of charisma— on hearing Dandridge sing, talent manager Earl Mills (played by Brent Spiner) announces, "Whoever sang that song, I'm gonna make her a star"— Dandridge's story mirrors the abuse, problematic relationships, and tragedy of star biopics like that of Garland, and fictional narratives including *A Star Is Born*, represented through the alternative experience of African American stardom. Therefore, though Dandridge's "discovery" occurs at a Hollywood party she attends alongside Marilyn Monroe and Ava Gardner, the film makes clear throughout that race defines and confines her star text (figure A.1). From *Variety* announcements of leading roles going to white stars Gardner and Audrey Hepburn to Darryl Zanuck's suggestion that "the public isn't ready for a colored leading lady," and a Las Vegas hotel's demand that Dandridge remain in her room when not performing (the hotel's pool is drained when she defiantly her toe in it), the narrative outlines the distinctions rather than similarities between black and normative white stardom, as defined by Hollywood and America's entertainment industry.

The film simultaneously represents Dandridge's significance in resisting the various humiliations of these everyday inequalities, as she challenges Zanuck on his sexualization of her as a black female star, demands the same salary as Gardner, and fights for starring roles. The film's highlighting of Dandridge's importance as a trailblazing star draws on commentary in the black press such as *Ebony* magazine, which profiled the star in 1962 in ways that both paralleled and disturbed the promotion of white female stars. Photographed in her home in the Hollywood Hills, Dandridge is described as "Hollywood's first authentic love goddess of color"[4] with an aura of mystique comparable to that of Greta Garbo.[5] Interjected

Fig. A.1: *Introducing Dorothy Dandridge* (HBO, 1999). Dorothy Dandridge (Halle Berry) is discovered beside Ava Gardner and Marilyn Monroe, but her experience of stardom will be vastly different.

amongst this familiar imagery are references to the significance of Dandridge's lead role, her Academy Award nomination for *Carmen Jones* (Otto Preminger, 1954) as the first such for an African American actor, her lawsuit against *Confidential* magazine for its false story of an assignation, and her comments on her increased workload in Europe that came as a result of limited opportunities in Hollywood for black actresses.[6]

In her acceptance speech on winning the Academy Award for her lead role in *Monster's Ball* (Marc Forster, 2001), Halle Berry positioned herself in the midst of a history of African American actresses who had not been so awarded, claiming the win on behalf of Dandridge, Lena Horne, Diahann Carroll, and several of her contemporaries. Her speech echoed her earlier comments on the release of *Introducing Dorothy Dandridge*, connecting herself to the star in a historicization of African American female stardom. As Berry referred to "supernatural occurrences" around her possession of one of Dandridge's personal gowns, she suggested that "this may be my ego or my fantasy, but I believe Dorothy passed the ball to me. And I say that with such strong feelings of responsibility and humility. She blazed a trail for Black actresses and fought so hard to widen horizons for our people. That's how I approach my career. I want to fight as hard as she did."[7]

These films and their infrequency illustrate Hollywood's construction of stardom through whiteness, inevitably resulting in the characterization through which the stardom film dramatizes the star myth. While depictions of African American stardom consistently draw on such mythology and the tropes of the dominant form of the stardom narrative, their explicit illumination of industry inequalities and an alternative experience of stardom repeatedly intervene in the star myth, disturbing its validity with this parallel Hollywood history. With the shifting contexts in American culture and the Hollywood film industry come pending projects reportedly in development, including a collaboration between Harry Belafonte and British director Steve McQueen for a feature-length Paul Robeson biopic and a Lee Daniels miniseries on the life of Sammy Davis Jr. through Tom Hanks's Playtone Productions. Such narratives promise the possibility of a redrawing of the star myth and of the stardom film genre through which we continue to understand this captivating and potent mythology.

NOTES

Introduction

1. Lucy Fischer, "Screen Test: Celebrity, the Starlet, and the Movie World in Silent American Cinema," *Feminist Media Histories* 2, no. 4 (Fall 2016): 15–63; Shelley Stamp, "'It's a Long Way to Filmland': Starlets, Screen Hopefuls, and Extras in Early Hollywood," in *American Cinema's Transitional Era: Audiences, Institutions, Practices*, ed. Charlie Keil and Shelley Stamp (Berkeley: University of California Press, 2004), 332–52.

2. J. E. Smyth, "Hollywood 'Takes One More Look': Early Histories of Silent Hollywood and the Fallen Star Biography, 1932–1937," *Historical Journal of Film, Radio and Television* 26, no. 2 (June 2006): 179–201.

3. Steven Cohan, *Hollywood by Hollywood: The Backstudio Picture and the Mystique of Making Movies* (New York: Oxford University Press, 2019).

4. Christopher Ames, *Movies About the Movies: Hollywood Reflected* (Lexington: University Press of Kentucky, 1997).

5. Alex Barris, *Hollywood According to Hollywood* (South Brunswick, NJ: A. S. Barnes and Company, 1978); Rudy Behlmer and Tony Thomas, *The Movies About the Movies: Hollywood's Hollywood* (Secaucus, NJ: Citadel Press, 1979); Richard Meyers, *Movies on Movies: How Hollywood Sees Itself* (New York: Drake, 1978); Anthony Slide, *Films on Film History* (Metuchen, NJ: Scarecrow Press, 1979).

6. Cohan, *Hollywood by Hollywood*, 2–3.

7. John Ellis, *Visible Fictions: Cinema, Television, Video* (London: Routledge, 1982), 91.

8. Edgar Morin, *The Stars: An Account of the Star-System in Motion Pictures* (New York: Grove Press, 1961), 39, https://archive.org/details/starsaccountofstoomori /page/n1/mode/2up.

9. Michael Williams, *Film Stardom, Myth and Classicism: The Rise of Hollywood's Gods* (Basingstoke, UK: Palgrave Macmillan, 2013), 16.
10. Frank S. Nugent, "Another Dance of the Seven Veils: The Screen Reveals Its Mysteries to the Public Yet Manages to Hide Behind the Cloak of Illusion," *New York Times*, October 10, 1937, 177.
11. Kevin Starr, *Inventing the Dream: California Through the Progressive Era* (New York: Oxford University Press, 1985), 334.
12. Lary May, *Screening Out the Past: The Birth of Mass Culture and the Motion Picture Industry* (New York: Oxford University Press, 1980), 189.
13. Fischer, "Screen Test," 19.

1. Core Stardom Narratives

1. Shelley Stamp, "'It's a Long Way to Filmland': Starlets, Screen Hopefuls, and Extras in Early Hollywood," in *American Cinema's Transitional Era: Audiences, Institutions, Practices*, ed. Charlie Keil and Shelley Stamp (Berkeley: University of California Press, 2004), 332–33.
2. Laurence A. Hughes, *The Truth About the Movies by the Stars* (Hollywood, CA: Hollywood Publishers, 1924), 63.
3. "A Foreword to *Souls for Sale* by Rupert Hughes," *Exhibitors Herald*, March 31, 1923, 32, https://archive.org/stream/exhibitorsherald16exhi_o#page/n51/mode/2up/search/souls+for+sale.
4. "A Foreword," 32.
5. "Goldwyn Sponsors Drive to Tell the Truth About Hollywood," *Exhibitors Herald*, April 21, 1923, 25, https://archive.org/stream/exhibitorsherald16exhi_o#page/n331/mode/2up/search/souls+for+sale.
6. *Motion Picture News*, July–August 1923, 667, https://archive.org/stream/motionpicturenewoomoti_2#page/n683/mode/2up/search/souls+for+sale; "Impersonation Stunt Used on 'Souls for Sale,'" *Motion Picture News*, July-August 1923, 536, https://archive.org/stream/motionpicturenewoomoti_2#page/n549/mode/2up/search/souls+for+sale; "Newspaper Tie-up Wins Space for *Souls for Sale* Run," *Motion Picture News*, July–August 1923, 288, https://archive.org/stream/motionpicturenewoomoti_2#page/n297/mode/2up/search/souls+for+sale.
7. Alma Whitaker, "'Don't Laugh *Here*': We No Longer Emote According to Rules, Says Alma Whitaker," *Screenland from Hollywood*, July 1923, 71, https://archive.org/stream/ScreenlandJuly1923#page/n69/mode/2up/search/souls+for+sale.
8. Michael Sragow, *Victor Fleming: An American Movie Master* (New York: Pantheon Books, 2008), 199.
9. Raymond Durgnat and Scott Simmon, *King Vidor, American* (Berkeley: University of California Press, 1988), 90.
10. Steve Neale and Frank Krutnik, *Popular Film and Television Comedy* (London: Routledge, 1990), 24.
11. Myrtle Gebhart, "Just a Hard-Woiking Goil!," *Picture Play*, March 1928, 53, https://archive.org/details/pictureplaymagaz28unse/page/n675.

12. Gebhart, "Hard-Woiking Goil!," 106.
13. Gebhart, "Hard-Woiking Goil!," 106.
14. Gebhart, "Hard-Woiking Goil!," 106.
15. Gebhart, "Hard-Woiking Goil!," 52.
16. Rudy Behlmer and Tony Thomas, *The Movies About the Movies: Hollywood's Hollywood* (Secaucus, NJ: Citadel Press, 1979), 111.
17. *Variety*, May 14, 1930, *Show Girl in Hollywood* Core Production Files, Margaret Herrick Library, Academy of Motion Picture Arts and Sciences.
18. *Variety*, May 14, 1930.
19. Chris Yogerst, *From the Headlines to Hollywood: The Birth and Boom of Warner Bros.* (Lanham, MD: Rowman & Littlefield, 2016), 6.
20. Nicholas Emme, "The Reality of Illusion: Self-Reflexivity in *Show Girl in Hollywood* (1930)," *Spectator* 33, no. 1 (Spring 2013): 41.
21. *Showgirl in Hollywood* promotional ad, *Picture Play*, June 1930, 14, https://archive.org/details/picturepl32stre/page/n651.
22. Emme, "The Reality of Illusion," 38.
23. Emme, "The Reality of Illusion," 42.
24. Dorothy Wooldridge, "It Might Have Been You," *Modern Screen*, September 1932, 26–27, 98–99, https://archive.org/stream/modernscreen34unse#page/n907/mode/2up.
25. Smyth, "Hollywood 'Takes One More Look,'" 181.
26. Smyth, "Hollywood 'Takes One More Look,'" 183–86.
27. Behlmer and Thomas, *The Movies About the Movies*, 76–77.
28. Smyth, "Hollywood 'Takes One More Look,'" 183; Behlmer and Thomas, *The Movies About the Movies*, 76.
29. Jackie Stacey, *Star Gazing: Hollywood Cinema and Female Spectatorship* (London: Routledge, 1994).
30. David Thomson, *Showman: The Life of David O. Selznick* (London: Abacus, 1993), 139.
31. Lee Carruthers, "Modulations of the Shot: The Quiet Film Style of George Cukor," in *George Cukor: Hollywood Master*, ed. Murray Pomerance and R. Barton Palmer (Edinburgh: Edinburgh University Press, 2015), 83.
32. Behlmer and Thomas, *The Movies About the Movies*, 81.
33. Smyth, "Hollywood 'Takes One More Look,'" 197.
34. Thomson, *Showman*, 226.
35. Thomson, *Showman*, 226.
36. Behlmer and Thomas, *The Movies About the Movies*, 81.
37. Axel Madsen, *Stanwyck: A Biography* (New York: HarperCollins, 1994), n.p.
38. Behlmer and Thomas, *The Movies About the Movies*, 82.
39. "Movie of the Week: A Star is Born," *Life*, May 3, 1937, 41; "Screenland Honor Page," *Screenland*, July 1937, 8, http://www.archive.org/stream/screenland35unse/screenland35unse#page/n207/mode/2up/search/screen+honor.
40. "Movie of the Week: A Star is Born," 41; "Screenland Honor Page," 8.
41. Dana Burnet, "Volcanic Hollywood," *Silver Screen*, August 1937, 19, https://archive.org/details/silverscreen07unse_0/page/n287/mode/2up.

42. Muriel Babcock, "She Knew What She Wanted," *Modern Screen*, October 1937, 36, https://archive.org/details/modernscreen1415unse/page/n945.

2. Genre and Hybridity

1. Steven Cohan, " 'Feminizing' the Song and Dance Man: Fred Astaire and the Spectacle of Masculinity in the Hollywood Musical," in *Hollywood Musicals, the Film Reader*, ed. Steven Cohan (London: Routledge, 2002), 87.

2. Jane Feuer, "The Self-Reflective Musical and the Myth of Entertainment," *Quarterly Review of Film Studies* 2, no. 3 (1977): 313–26.

3. Gerald Mast, *Can't Help Singin': The American Musical on Stage and Screen* (Woodstock, NY: The Overlook Press, 1987), 264.

4. Jane Feuer, "The Self-Reflective Musical and the Myth of Entertainment," 315–19.

5. Mast, *Can't Help Singin'*, 264.

6. Steven Cohan, *Hollywood by Hollywood: The Backstudio Picture and the Mystique of Making Movies* (New York: Oxford University Press, 2019), 131.

7. "*Singin' in the Rain*," Collection Highlights, Oscars.org, http://www.oscars.org /collection-highlights/singin-rain/.

8. Warner Bros. Studios, "Production Notes on 'A Star is Born' (1954)," Harry B. Friedman Collection, Special Collections, Margaret Herrick Library, Academy of Motion Picture Arts and Sciences.

9. Ronald Haver, *A Star Is Born: The Making of the 1954 Movie and Its 1983 Restoration* (New York: Alfred A. Knopf, 1988).

10. Cohan, *Hollywood by Hollywood*, 120.

11. Warner Bros. Studios, "Production Notes on 'A Star is Born' (1954)."

12. Short feature story 9–1251, *A Star Is Born* (1954) folder, Harry B. Friedman Collection, Special Collections, Margaret Herrick Library, Academy of Motion Picture Arts and Sciences.

13. Warner Bros. Studios, "Production Notes on 'A Star is Born' (1954)."

14. *A Star Is Born* (1954) folder, George Cukor Collection, Special Collections, Margaret Herrick Library, Academy of Motion Picture Arts and Sciences.

15. "Discuss with Moss Hart," typed notes, September 17, 1953, *A Star Is Born* (1954) folder, George Cukor Collection, Special Collections, Margaret Herrick Library, Academy of Motion Picture Arts and Sciences.

16. Lorna Luft and Jeffrey Vance, *A Star Is Born: Judy Garland and the Film That Got Away* (New York: Running Press, 2018), 109.

17. Warner Bros. Studios, "Production Notes on 'A Star is Born' (1954)."

18. Warner Bros. Studios, "Production Notes on 'A Star is Born' (1954)."

19. *A Star Is Born, Judy Garland: The Signature Collection DVD Box Set*, Warner Bros. (2009).

20. Warner Bros. press release to the *New York Times*, *A Star Is Born* (1954) folder, Harry B. Friedman Collection, Special Collections, Margaret Herrick Library, Academy of Motion Picture Arts and Sciences.

21. George Cukor's blue pages of final script additions and changes, October 16, 1953, *A Star Is Born* (1954) folder, George Cukor Collection, Special Collections, Margaret Herrick Library, Academy of Motion Picture Arts and Sciences.

22. Luft and Vance, *A Star Is Born*, 29.

23. Warner Bros. press release to the *New York Times*, *A Star Is Born* (1954) folder, Harry B. Friedman Collection, Special Collections, Margaret Herrick Library, Academy of Motion Picture Arts and Sciences.

24. Shaun Considine, *Bette and Joan: The Divine Feud* (London: Sphere Books, 1990), 261.

25. Considine, *Bette and Joan*, 262.

26. Brooks Atkinson, "Case of Bette Davis: A Dramatic Actress of the Screen Turns Leading Performer in a Stage Revue," *New York Times*, December 21, 1952.

27. Karen Beckman, *Vanishing Women: Magic, Film, and Feminism* (Durham, NC: Duke University Press, 2003), 162.

28. Christopher Ames, *Movies About the Movies: Hollywood Reflected* (Lexington: University Press of Kentucky, 1997), 42.

29. Considine, *Bette and Joan*, 262.

30. Bosley Crowther, "More About Hollywood: Bette Davis Plays a Movie Has-Been in 'The Star,'" *New York Times*, February 1, 1953.

31. "Movies—'Sunset Boulevard': Hollywood Tale That Gloria Swanson Makes Great," *Newsweek*, June 26, 1950, 82–84, Paramount Pictures Production Records *Sunset Boulevard*, Clippings and Reviews Folder, Special Collections, Margaret Herrick Library, Academy of Motion Picture Arts and Sciences.

32. Pat Kirkham, "Saul Bass and Billy Wilder in Conversation," in *Billy Wilder Interviews*, ed. Robert Horton (Jackson: University Press of Mississippi, 2001), 179. Originally published in *Sight and Sound*, June 1995.

33. Lucy Fischer, "*Sunset Boulevard*: Fading Stars," in *Women and Film*, ed. Janet Todd (New York: Holmes and Meier, 1988), 103.

34. Alan Nadel, *Demographic Angst: Cultural Narratives and American Films of the 1950s* (New Brunswick, NJ: Rutgers University Press, 2018), 70.

35. Nadel, *Demographic Angst*, 69.

36. Anthony Slide, ed., *"It's the Pictures That Got Small": Charles Brackett on Billy Wilder and Hollywood's Golden Age* (New York: Columbia University Press, 2015), 367.

37. Slide, *"It's the Pictures That Got Small,"* 378.

38. Anne Morey, "Grotesquerie as Marker of Success in Aging Female Stars," in *In the Limelight and Under the Microscope: Forms and Functions of Female Celebrity*, ed. Su Holmes and Diane Negra (New York: Continuum, 2011), 108.

39. Bette Davis interviewed by Joan Bakewell, National Film Theatre, 1972, in *Talking Pictures*, BBC2, June 10, 2017, https://www.bbc.co.uk/programmes/b01ps8jc.

40. Beckman, *Vanishing Women*, 162.

41. Bosley Crowther, "Screen: Bette Davis and Joan Crawford," *New York Times*, October 7, 1962, 48, *What Ever Happened to Baby Jane* Core Production Files, Margaret Herrick Library, Academy of Motion Picture Arts and Sciences.

42. James Powers, "What Ever Happened to Baby Jane Review," *Hollywood Reporter*, October 26, 1962, *What Ever Happened to Baby Jane* Core Production Files, Margaret Herrick Library, Academy of Motion Picture Arts and Sciences.

43. Bette Davis interviewed by François Chalais, Cannes Film Festival, May 16, 1963, *Qu'est-il arrive à Bette Davis?*, https://fresques.ina.fr/festival-de-cannes-fr/fiche -media/Cannes00084/bette-davis-en-competition.html.

44. *The Jack Paar Show*, NBC, November 16, 1962.

45. *The Andy Williams Show*, NBC, December 20, 1962.

46. Bette Davis interviewed by François Chalais.

47. Cohan, *Hollywood by Hollywood*, 217–22.

3. Character, Star, and Myth

1. Christopher Ames, *Movies About the Movies: Hollywood Reflected* (Lexington: University Press of Kentucky, 1997), 109–10.

2. Tony Williams, *Body and Soul: The Cinematic Vision of Robert Aldrich* (Lanham, MD: Scarecrow Press, 2004), 204.

3. Karen McNally, " 'Have They Forgotten What a Star Looks Like?' Image and Theme with Dino, Cagney, and Fedora," in *Billy Wilder, Movie-Maker*, ed. Karen McNally (Jefferson, NC: McFarland & Co., 2011), 87–101.

4. Mary Blume, "Walking on the Wilder Side," *Los Angeles Times*, October 2, 1977, *Fedora* Core Production Files, Margaret Herrick Library, Academy of Motion Picture Arts and Sciences.

5. Rex McGee, "The Life and Hard Times of *Fedora*: And the Trials and Tribulations Billy Wilder Faced in Filming the Tale of a Legendary Star," *American Film*, February 1979, 19, Production Material for *Fedora* folder, Special Collections, Margaret Herrick Library, Academy of Motion Picture Arts and Sciences.

6. "*Fedora* Review," *New Republic*, May 5, 1979, *Fedora* Core Production Files, Margaret Herrick Library, Academy of Motion Picture Arts and Sciences.

7. Stephen Farber, "Magnificent Obsession," *New West*, May 7, 1979, 84, *Fedora* Core Production Files, Margaret Herrick Library, Academy of Motion Picture Arts and Sciences.

8. "Notes for 'Rain for the Contessa,' " Notes commencing January 2, 1952, *The Barefoot Contessa* Production Files—Produced, Joseph L. Mankiewicz Papers, Special Collections, Margaret Herrick Library, Academy of Motion Picture Arts and Sciences.

9. Ava Gardner, *Ava: My Story* (London: Bantam Press, 1990), 195; Peter Evans and Ava Gardner, *Ava Gardner: The Secret Conversations* (London: Simon & Schuster, 2013), 63.

10. *Newsweek*, October 4, 1954, n.p., *The Barefoot Contessa* Core Production Files, Margaret Herrick Library, Academy of Motion Picture Arts and Sciences.

11. Letter from Joseph L. Mankiewicz to Michael Waszynski, September 28, 1953, *The Barefoot Contessa* Production Files, Joseph L. Mankiewicz Papers, Special Collections, Margaret Herrick Library, Academy of Motion Picture Arts and Sciences.

12. Letter from Joseph L. Mankiewicz to Michael Waszynski, September 28, 1953.

13. Letters from Bert Allenberg to Joseph L. Mankiewicz, April 30, 1953; May 15, 1953; June 23, 1953; July 8, 1953; October 16, 1953; *The Barefoot Contessa*—William Morris (Mankiewicz) Folder, Joseph L. Mankiewicz Papers, Special Collections, Margaret Herrick Library, Academy of Motion Picture Arts and Sciences.

14. Letter from Joseph L. Mankiewicz to Bert Allenberg, July 14, 1953; Letters from Bert Allenberg to Joseph L. Mankiewicz, June 23, 1953, December 22, 1953, *The Barefoot Contessa*—William Morris (Mankiewicz) Folder, Joseph L. Mankiewicz Papers, Special Collections, Margaret Herrick Library, Academy of Motion Picture Arts and Sciences.

15. Letter from Bert Allenberg to Joseph L. Mankiewicz, June 26, 1953; Letter from Joseph L. Mankiewicz to Bert Allenberg, July 14, 1953, *The Barefoot Contessa*—William Morris (Mankiewicz) Folder, Joseph L. Mankiewicz Papers, Special Collections, Margaret Herrick Library, Academy of Motion Picture Arts and Sciences.

16. Letters from Bert Allenberg to Joseph L. Mankiewicz, October 27, 1953, October 30, 1953, *The Barefoot Contessa*—William Morris (Mankiewicz) Folder, Joseph L. Mankiewicz Papers, Special Collections, Margaret Herrick Library, Academy of Motion Picture Arts and Sciences.

17. Susan Felleman, *Art and the Cinematic Imagination* (Austin: University of Texas Press, 2006), 59.

18. Letter from Joseph L. Mankiewicz to Bert Allenberg, June 12, 1953; Letter from Bert Allenberg to Joseph L. Mankiewicz, June 23, 1953; Western Union telegram from Bert Allenberg to Joseph L. Mankiewicz, October 22, 1953, *The Barefoot Contessa*—William Morris (Mankiewicz) Folder, Joseph L. Mankiewicz Papers, Special Collections, Margaret Herrick Library, Academy of Motion Picture Arts and Sciences.

19. Felleman, *Art and the Cinematic Imagination*, 57–58.

20. *Harper's Bazaar*, November 1954, n.p., *The Barefoot Contessa* Core Production Files, Margaret Herrick Library, Academy of Motion Picture Arts and Sciences.

21. Evelyn Harvey, "Ava Gardner Plays the *Gypsy*," *Colliers*, July 23, 1954, 28–29, *The Barefoot Contessa* Core Production Files, Margaret Herrick Library, Academy of Motion Picture Arts and Sciences.

22. Gardner, *Ava*, 197.

23. Gardner, *Ava*, 200.

24. Letter from Joseph L. Mankiewicz to Bert Allenberg, December 15, 1953, *The Barefoot Contessa*—William Morris (Mankiewicz) Folder, Joseph L. Mankiewicz Papers, Margaret Herrick Library, Academy of Motion Picture Arts and Sciences.

25. "Notes for 'Rain for the Contessa,'" notes commencing January 2, 1952, *The Barefoot Contessa* Production Files—Produced, Joseph L. Mankiewicz Papers, Special Collections, Margaret Herrick Library, Academy of Motion Picture Arts and Sciences.

26. Dick Williams, "Hollywood Peers at Itself Again," *Mirror News*, May 3, 1958, n.p., *The Goddess* Core Production Files, Margaret Herrick Library, Academy of Motion Picture Arts and Sciences.

27. Philip K. Scheuer, "Kim Stanley: Star Is Born," *Los Angeles Times*, May 2, 1958, n.p., *The Goddess* Core Production Files, Margaret Herrick Library, Academy of Motion Picture Arts and Sciences.

28. Steven Cohan, *Hollywood by Hollywood: The Backstudio Picture and the Mystique of Making Movies* (New York: Oxford University Press, 2019), 135.

29. Dennis Bingham, *Whose Lives Are They Anyway? The Biopic as Contemporary Film Genre* (New Brunswick: Rutgers University Press, 2010), 5.

30. Jean-Louis Comolli, "Historical Fiction: A Body Too Much," *Screen* vol. 19, no. 2 (Summer 1978), 44.

31. George F. Custen, *Bio/Pics* (New Brunswick: Rutgers University Press, 1992), 170.

32. Teletext from Bevedit Zeitlin to Will Lang for Tommy Thompson, David I. Zeitlin Papers—Jean Harlow, Special Collections, Margaret Herrick Library, Academy of Motion Picture Arts and Sciences.

33. A. T. McKenna, "*Harlow*'s Bridle, or How Avoiding Sex and Engaging the Competition Can Lead to Failure," *Journal of Popular Film and Television* 38, no. 1 (2010): 34–43.

34. Philip K. Scheuer, "A Behind the Scenes Look at What Makes *Oscar* Run," *Los Angeles Times Calendar*, September 12, 1965, quoted in McKenna, "*Harlow*'s Bridle," 37.

35. John T. Elson, "Two Harlows – Deluxe and Quickie," *Life*, May 7, 1965, 122.

36. Elson, "Two Harlows," 122.

37. Steven Cohan, "This Industry Lives on Gossip and Scandal: Female Star Narratives and the Marilyn Monroe Biopic," *Celebrity Studies* 7, no. 4 (2017): 7–8.

38. Elson, "Two Harlows," 118.

39. Toby Chamberlain, "Glamour Recreated by Fashion Trend Harlow Epic," *Western Apparel Industry*, May 1965, Edith Head Papers—*Harlow* Clippings Folder, Special Collections, Margaret Herrick Library, Academy of Motion Picture Arts and Sciences.

40. *Daily Variety*, June 22, 1965, n.p., Edith Head Papers—*Harlow* Reviews Folder, Special Collections, Margaret Herrick Library, Academy of Motion Picture Arts and Sciences.

41. Howard Thompson, "Screen: Winner of the 'Harlow' Race: Carol Lynley Is Cast as Late Actress," *New York Times*, May 15, 1965, http://nytimes.com/1965/05/15/archives/screen-winner-of-the-harlow-racecarol-lynley-is-cast-as-late.html.

42. Clarus Backes, "Levine Film of Harlow Has Flash—Lots of It," *Chicago Tribune*, June 26, 1965, Edith Head Papers—*Harlow* Reviews File, Special Collections, Margaret Herrick Library, Academy of Motion Picture Arts and Sciences.

43. Cohan, "This Industry Lives on Gossip and Scandal," 4.

44. Custen, *Bio/Pics*, 174.

45. Cohan, *Hollywood by Hollywood*, 212.

46. Sarah Churchwell, *The Many Lives of Marilyn Monroe* (London: Picador, 2004), 3; Cohan, *Hollywood by Hollywood*, 212–17.

47. Sam Wollaston, "TV Review: Burton and Taylor," *Guardian*, July 22, 2013, https://www.theguardian.com/tv-and-radio/2013/jul/22/burton-taylor-twisters-tv-review.

48. Tim Goodman, "Liz & Dick: TV Review," *Hollywood Reporter*, November 16, 2012, https://www.hollywoodreporter.com/review/lindsay-lohan-liz-dick-tv-391316.
49. Judy Garland interviewed by Barbara Walters, *Today*, NBC, March 16, 1967.
50. Lorna Luft, *Me and My Shadows: A Family Memoir* (New York: Simon & Schuster, 1998).
51. Guy Lodge, "Renée Zellweger in 'Judy,'" *Variety*, August 30, 2019, https://variety.com/2019/film/reviews/judy-review-renee-zellweger-1203316871/.
52. Lodge, "Renée Zellweger in 'Judy.'"
53. Richard Brody, "'Judy,' Reviewed: Renée Zellweger's Transcendent Performance as Judy Garland," *New Yorker*, September 25, 2019, https://www.newyorker.com/culture/the-front-row/judy-reviewed-renee-zellwegers-transcendent-performance-as-judy-garland.

Afterword

1. Thomas Doherty, "Malcolm X: In Print, On Screen," *Biography* 23, no. 1 (Winter 2000): 37.
2. Jennifer Fuller, "Branding Blackness on US Cable Television," *Media, Culture & Society* 32, no. 2 (2010): 287.
3. Fuller, "Branding Blackness," 287.
4. Louie Robinson, "The Private World of Dorothy Dandridge," *Ebony*, June 1962, 117.
5. Robinson, "Dorothy Dandridge," 120.
6. Robinson, "Dorothy Dandridge," 116–21.
7. Laura B. Randolph, "Halle Berry on How She Found Dorothy Dandridge's Spirit— And Finally Healed Her Own," *Ebony*, August 1999, 94.

BIBLIOGRAPHY

Ames, Christopher. *Movies About the Movies: Hollywood Reflected.* Lexington: University Press of Kentucky, 1997.

Atkinson, Brooks. "Case of Bette Davis: A Dramatic Actress of the Screen Turns Leading Performer in a Stage Revue." *New York Times,* December 21, 1952.

Babcock, Muriel. "She Knew What She Wanted." *Modern Screen,* October 1937, 36–27, 80–82. https://archive.org/details/modernscreen1415unse/page/n945.

Backes, Clarus. "Levinde Film of Harlow Has Flash—Lots of It." *Chicago Tribune,* June 26, 1965. Edith Head Papers—Harlow Reviews File. Special Collections, Margaret Herrick Library, Academy of Motion Picture Arts and Sciences.

Barris, Alex. *Hollywood According to Hollywood.* South Brunswick, NJ: A. S. Barnes and Company, 1978.

Beckman, Karen. *Vanishing Women: Magic, Film, and Feminism.* Durham, NC: Duke University Press, 2003.

Behlmer, Rudy, and Tony Thomas. *The Movies About the Movies: Hollywood's Hollywood.* Secaucus, NJ: Citadel Press, 1979.

Bingham, Dennis. *Whose Lives Are They Anyway? The Biopic as Contemporary Film Genre.* New Brunswick, NJ: Rutgers University Press, 2010.

Blume, Mary. "Walking on the Wilder Side." *Los Angeles Times,* October 2, 1977. *Fedora* Core Production Files, Margaret Herrick Library, Academy of Motion Picture Arts and Sciences.

Brody, Richard. "'Judy,' Reviewed: Renée Zellweger's Transcendent Performance as Judy Garland." *New Yorker,* September 25, 2019. https://www.newyorker.com/culture/the-front-row/judy-reviewed-renee-zellwegers-transcendent-performance-as-judy-garland.

Burnet, Dana. "Volcanic Hollywood." *Silver Screen,* August 1937, 18–19, 75. https://archive.org/details/silverscreen07unse_0/page/n287/mode/2up.

Carruthers, Lee. "Modulations of the Shot: The Quiet Film Style of George Cukor." In *George Cukor: Hollywood Master*, ed. Murray Pomerance and R. Barton Palmer, 77–91. Edinburgh: Edinburgh University Press, 2015.

Chamberlain, Toby. "Glamour Recreated by Fashion Trend Harlow Epic." *Western Apparel Industry*, May 1965. Edith Head Papers—*Harlow* Clippings Folder. Special Collections, Margaret Herrick Library, Academy of Motion Picture Arts and Sciences.

Churchwell, Sarah. *The Many Lives of Marilyn Monroe*. London: Picador, 2004.

Cohan, Steven. "'Feminizing' the Song and Dance Man: Fred Astaire and the Spectacle of Masculinity in the Hollywood Musical." In *Hollywood Musicals, the Film Reader*, ed. Steven Cohan, 87–102. London: Routledge, 2002.

Cohan, Steven. *Hollywood by Hollywood: The Backstudio Picture and the Mystique of Making Movies*. New York: Oxford University Press, 2019.

Cohan, Steven. "This Industry Lives on Gossip and Scandal: Female Star Narratives and the Marilyn Monroe Biopic." *Celebrity Studies* 7, no. 4 (2017): 527–43.

Comolli, Jean-Louis. "Historical Fiction: A Body Too Much." *Screen* 19, no. 2 (Summer 1978): 41–54.

Considine, Shaun. *Bette and Joan: The Divine Feud*. London: Sphere Books, 1990.

Crowther, Bosley. "More About Hollywood: Bette Davis Plays a Movie Has-Been in 'The Star.'" *New York Times*, February 1, 1953.

Crowther, Bosley. "Screen: Bette Davis and Joan Crawford." *New York Times*, October 7, 1962, 48. *What Ever Happened to Baby Jane?* Core Production Files, Margaret Herrick Library, Academy of Motion Picture Arts and Sciences.

Cukor, George. Blue pages of final script additions and changes, October 16, 1953. *A Star Is Born* (1954) folder. George Cukor Collection, Special Collections, Margaret Herrick Library, Academy of Motion Picture Arts and Sciences.

Custen, George F. *Bio/Pics*. New Brunswick, NJ: Rutgers University Press, 1992.

Daily Variety, June 22, 1965. Edith Head Papers—*Harlow* Reviews Folder. Special Collections, Margaret Herrick Library, Academy of Motion Picture Arts and Sciences.

Davis, Bette. Interview by Joan Bakewell. National Film Theatre, 1972. In *Talking Pictures*, BBC2, June 10, 2017. https://www.bbc.co.uk/programmes/bo1ps8jc.

Davis, Bette. Interview by François Chalais. Cannes Film Festival, May 16, 1963. *Qu'est-il arrive à Bette Davis?* https://fresques.ina.fr/festival-de-cannes-fr/fiche-media/Cannes00084/bette-davis-en-competition.html.

"Discuss with Moss Hart." Typed notes, September 17, 1953. *A Star Is Born* (1954) folder. George Cukor Collection, Special Collections, Margaret Herrick Library, Academy of Motion Picture Arts and Sciences.

Doherty, Thomas. "Malcolm X: In Print, On Screen," *Biography* 23, no. 1 (Winter 2000): 29–48.

Durgnat, Raymond, and Scott Simmon. *King Vidor, American*. Berkeley: University of California Press, 1988.

John Ellis, *Visible Fictions: Cinema, Television, Video*. London: Routledge, 1982.

Elson, John T. "Two Harlows—Deluxe and Quickie." *Life*, May 7, 1965, 122.

Emme, Nicholas. "The Reality of Illusion: Self-Reflexivity in *Show Girl in Hollywood* (1930)." *Spectator* 33, no. 1 (Spring 2013): 36–44.

Evans, Peter, and Ava Gardner. *Ava Gardner: The Secret Conversations*. London: Simon & Schuster, 2013.

Farber, Stephen. "Magnificent Obsession." *New West*, May 7, 1979, 83–87. *Fedora* Core Production Files, Margaret Herrick Library, Academy of Motion Picture Arts and Sciences.

"*Fedora* Review." *New Republic*, May 5, 1979. *Fedora* Core Production Files, Margaret Herrick Library, Academy of Motion Picture Arts and Sciences.

Felleman, Susan. *Art and the Cinematic Imagination*. Austin: University of Texas Press.

Feuer, Jane. "The Self-Reflective Musical and the Myth of Entertainment." *Quarterly Review of Film Studies* 2, no. 3 (1977): 313–26.

Fischer, Lucy. "Screen Test: Celebrity, the Starlet, and the Movie World in Silent American Cinema." *Feminist Media Histories* (Fall 2016): 15–63.

Fischer, Lucy. "*Sunset Boulevard*: Fading Stars." In *Women and Film*, ed. Janet Todd, 97–113. New York: Holmes and Meier, 1988.

"A Foreword to *Souls for Sale* by Rupert Hughes." *Exhibitors Herald,* March 31, 1923: 32. https://archive.org/stream/exhibitorsherald16exhi_0#page/n51/mode/2up /search/souls+for+sale.

Fuller, Jennifer. "Branding Blackness on US Cable Television," *Media, Culture & Society* 32, no. 2 (2010): 285–305.

Gardner, Ava. *Ava: My Story*. London: Bantam Press, 1990.

Garland, Judy. Interview by Barbara Walters. *Today*, NBC, March 16, 1967.

Gebhart, Myrtle. "Just a Hard-Woiking Goil!" *Picture Play*, March 1928, 52–53, 106. https://archive.org/details/pictureplaymagaz28unse/page/n675.

"Goldwyn Sponsors Drive to Tell the Truth About Hollywood." *Exhibitors Herald*, April 21, 1923, 25. https://archive.org/stream/exhibitorsherald16exhi_0#page /n331/mode/2up/search/souls+for+sale.

Goodman, Tim. "Liz & Dick: TV Review." *Hollywood Reporter*, November 16, 2012. https://www.hollywoodreporter.com/review/lindsay-lohan-liz-dick-tv-391316.

Harper's Bazaar, November 1954. *The Barefoot Contessa* Core Production Files, Margaret Herrick Library, Academy of Motion Picture Arts and Sciences.

Harvey, Evelyn. "Ava Gardner Plays the *Gypsy*." *Colliers*, July 23, 1954, 28–29. *The Barefoot Contessa* Core Production Files, Margaret Herrick Library, Academy of Motion Picture Arts and Sciences.

Haver, Ronald. *A Star Is Born: The Making of the 1954 Movie and Its 1983 Restoration*. New York: Alfred A. Knopf, 1988.

Hughes, Laurence A. *The Truth About the Movies by the Stars*. Hollywood, CA: Hollywood Publishers, 1924.

"Impersonation Stunt Used on Souls for Sale." *Motion Picture News*, July–August 1923, 536. https://archive.org/stream/motionpicturenewoomoti_2#page/n549/mode/2up /search/souls+for+sale

Kirkham, Pat. "Saul Bass and Billy Wilder in Conversation." In *Billy Wilder Interviews*, ed. Robert Horton, 171–81. Jackson: University Press of Mississippi, 2001. Originally published in *Sight and Sound*, June 1995.

Letters from Bert Allenberg to Joseph L. Mankiewicz, April 30, 1953; May 15, 1953; June 23, 1953; June 26, 1953; July 8, 1953; October 16, 1953; October 27, 1953; October 30, 1953; December 22, 1953. *The Barefoot Contessa*—William Morris (Mankiewicz) Folder. Joseph L. Mankiewicz Papers, Special Collections, Margaret Herrick Library, Academy of Motion Picture Arts and Sciences.

Letters from Joseph L. Mankiewicz to Bert Allenberg, June 12, 1953; July 14, 1953; December 15, 1953. *The Barefoot Contessa*—William Morris (Mankiewicz) Folder. Joseph L. Mankiewicz Papers, Special Collections, Margaret Herrick Library, Academy of Motion Picture Arts and Sciences.

Letter from Joseph L. Mankiewicz to Michael Waszynski, September 28, 1953. *The Barefoot Contessa* Production Files. Joseph L. Mankiewicz Papers, Special Collections, Margaret Herrick Library, Academy of Motion Picture Arts and Sciences.

Lodge, Guy. "Renée Zellweger in 'Judy.'" *Variety*, August 30, 2019. https://variety.com/2019/film/reviews/judy-review-renee-zellweger-1203316871/.

Luft, Lorna. *Me and My Shadows: A Family Memoir*. New York: Simon & Schuster, 1998.

Luft, Lorna, and Jeffrey Vance. *A Star Is Born: Judy Garland and the Film That Got Away*. New York: Running Press, 2018.

McGee, Rex. "The Life and Hard Times of *Fedora*: And the Trials and Tribulations Billy Wilder Faced in Filming the Tale of a Legendary Star." *American Film*, February 1979, 17–32. Production Material for *Fedora* folder. Special Collections, Margaret Herrick Library, Academy of Motion Picture Arts and Sciences.

McKenna, A. T. "*Harlow*'s Bridle, or How Avoiding Sex and Engaging the Competition Can Lead to Failure." *Journal of Popular Film and Television* 38, no. 1 (2010): 34–43.

McNally, Karen. "'Have They Forgotten What a Star Looks Like?' Image and Theme with Dino, Cagney and Fedora." In *Billy Wilder, Movie-Maker*, ed. Karen McNally, 87–101. Jefferson, NC: McFarland, 2011.

Madsen, Axel. *Stanwyck: A Biography*. New York: HarperCollins, 1994.

Mast, Gerald. *Can't Help Singin': The American Musical on Stage and Screen*. Woodstock, NY: The Overlook Press, 1987.

May, Lary. *Screening Out the Past: The Birth of Mass Culture and the Motion Picture Industry*. New York: Oxford University Press, 1980.

Meyers, Richard. *Movies on Movies: How Hollywood Sees Itself*. New York: Drake, 1978.

Morey, Anne. "Grotesquerie as Marker of Success in Aging Female Stars." In *In the Limelight and Under the Microscope: Forms and Functions of Female Celebrity*, ed. Su Holmes and Diane Negra, 103–24. New York: Continuum, 2011.

Morin, Edgar. *The Stars: An Account of the Star-System in Motion Pictures* (New York: Grove Press, 1961), 39. First published 1957. https://archive.org/details/starsaccount ofstoomori/page/n1/mode/2up.

Motion Picture News, July–August 1923, 667. https://archive.org/stream/motionpicture newoomoti_2#page/n683/mode/2up/search/souls+for+sale.

"Movie of the Week: A Star Is Born." *Life*, May 3, 1937, 41.

"Movies—'Sunset Boulevard': Hollywood Tale That Gloria Swanson Makes Great." *Newsweek*, June 26, 1950, 82–84. Paramount Pictures Production Records. *Sunset Boulevard*, Clippings and Reviews Folder. Special Collections, Margaret Herrick Library, Academy of Motion Picture Arts and Sciences.

Nadel, Alan. *Demographic Angst: Cultural Narratives and American Films of the 1950s*. New Brunswick, NJ: Rutgers University Press, 2018.

Neale, Steve, and Frank Krutnik. *Popular Film and Television Comedy*. London: Routledge, 1990.

"Newspaper Tie-up Wins Space for *Souls for Sale* Run." *Motion Picture News*, July–August 1923, 288. https://archive.org/stream/motionpicturenewoomoti_2#page/n297/mode/2up/search/souls+for+sale.

Newsweek, October 4, 1954. *The Barefoot Contessa* Core Production Files, Margaret Herrick Library, Academy of Motion Picture Arts and Sciences.

"Notes for 'Rain for the Contessa.' " Notes commencing January 2, 1952. *The Barefoot Contessa* Production Files—Produced. Joseph L. Mankiewicz Papers, Special Collections, Margaret Herrick Library, Academy of Motion Picture Arts and Sciences.

Nugent, Frank S. "Another Dance of the Seven Veils: The Screen Reveals Its Mysteries to the Public Yet Manages to Hide Behind the Cloak of Illusion." *New York Times*, October 10, 1937, 177.

Oscars.org. "Collection Highlights: *Signin' in the Rain*." http://www.oscars.org/collection-highlights/singin-rain/.

Picture Play, June 1930, 14. https://archive.org/details/picturepl32stre/page/n651.

Powers, James. "What Ever Happened to Baby Jane Review." *Hollywood Reporter*, October 26, 1962. *What Ever Happened to Baby Jane?* Core Production Files, Margaret Herrick Library, Academy of Motion Picture Arts and Sciences.

Randolph, Laura B. "Halle Berry on How She Found Dorothy Dandridge's Spirit—And Finally Healed Her Own." *Ebony*, August 1999, 90–91, 94, 96, 98.

Robinson, Louie. "The Private World of Dorothy Dandridge." *Ebony*, June 1962: 116–21.

Scheuer, Philip K. "Kim Stanley: Star is Born." *Los Angeles Times*, May 2, 1958. *The Goddess* Core Production Files, Margaret Herrick Library, Academy of Motion Picture Arts and Sciences.

"Screenland Honor Page." *Screenland*, July 1937, 8. http://www.archive.org/stream/screenland35unse/screenland35unse#page/n207/mode/2up/search/screen+honor.

Short feature story 9–1251. *A Star Is Born* (1954) folder. Harry B. Friedman Collection, Special Collections, Margaret Herrick Library, Academy of Motion Picture Arts and Sciences.

Slide, Anthony. *Films on Film History*. Metuchen, NJ: Scarecrow Press, 1979.

Slide, Anthony, ed. *"It's the Pictures That Got Small": Charles Brackett on Billy Wilder and Hollywood's Golden Age*. New York: Columbia University Press, 2015.

Smyth, J. E. "Hollywood 'Takes One More Look': Early Histories of Silent Hollywood and the Fallen Star Biography, 1932–1937." *Historical Journal of Film, Radio and Television* 26, no. 2 (June 2006): 179–201.

Sragow, Michael. *Victor Fleming: An American Movie Master.* New York: Pantheon Books, 2008.

Stacey, Jackie. *Star Gazing: Hollywood Cinema and Female Spectatorship.* London: Routledge, 1994.

Stamp, Shelley. "'It's a Long Way to Filmland': Starlets, Screen Hopefuls, and Extras in Early Hollywood." In *American Cinema's Transitional Era: Audiences, Institutions, Practices,* ed. Charlie Keil and Shelley Stamp, 332–52. Berkeley: University of California Press, 2004.

A Star Is Born (1954) folder. George Cukor Collection, Special Collections, Margaret Herrick Library, Academy of Motion Picture Arts and Sciences.

Starr, Kevin. *Inventing the Dream: California Through the Progressive Era.* New York: Oxford University Press, 1985.

Teletext from Bevedit Zeitlin to Will Lang for Tommy Thompson. David I. Zeitlin Papers—Jean Harlow. Special Collections, Margaret Herrick Library, Academy of Motion Picture Arts and Sciences.

Thompson, Howard. "Screen: Winner of the "Harlow" Race: Carol Lynley is Cast as Late Actress." *New York Times,* May 15, 1965. http://nytimes.com//1965/05/15/archives/screen-winner-of-the-harlow-racecarol-lynley-is-cast-as-late.html.

Thomson, David. *Showman: The Life of David O. Selznick.* London: Abacus, 1993.

Variety, May 14, 1930. *Show Girl in Hollywood* Core Production Files, Margaret Herrick Library, Academy of Motion Picture Arts and Sciences.

Warner Bros. Studios. *New York Times* press release, *A Star Is Born* (1954). Harry B. Friedman Collection, Special Collections, Margaret Herrick Library, Academy of Motion Picture Arts and Sciences.

Warner Bros. Studios. "Production Notes on 'A Star is Born' (1954)." Harry B. Friedman Collection, Special Collections, Margaret Herrick Library, Academy of Motion Picture Arts and Sciences.

Western Union telegram from Bert Allenberg to Joseph L. Mankiewicz, October 22, 1953. *The Barefoot Contessa*—William Morris (Mankiewicz) Folder. Joseph L. Mankiewicz Papers, Special Collections, Margaret Herrick Library, Academy of Motion Picture Arts and Sciences.

Whitaker, Alma. "'Don't Laugh *Here*': We No Longer Emote According to Rules says Alma Whitaker." *Screenland from Hollywood,* July 1923, 71. https://archive.org/stream/ScreenlandJuly1923#page/n69/mode/2up/search/souls+for+sale.

Williams, Dick. "Hollywood Peers at Itself Again." *Mirror News,* May 3, 1958. *The Goddess* Core Production Files, Margaret Herrick Library, Academy of Motion Picture Arts and Sciences.

Williams, Michael. *Film Stardom, Myth and Classicism: The Rise of Hollywood's Gods.* Basingstoke, UK: Palgrave Macmillan, 2013.

Williams, Tony. *Body and Soul: The Cinematic Vision of Robert Aldrich.* Lanham, MD: Scarecrow Press, 2004.

Wollaston, Sam. "TV Review: Burton and Taylor." *Guardian,* July 22, 2013. https://www.theguardian.com/tv-and-radio/2013/jul/22/burton-taylor-twisters-tv-review.

Wooldridge, Dorothy. "It Might Have Been You." *Modern Screen*, September 1932: 26–27, 98–99. https://archive.org/stream/modernscreen34unse#page/n907/mode/2up.

Yogerst, Chris. *From the Headlines to Hollywood: The Birth and Boom of Warner Bros.* Lanham, MD: Rowman & Littlefield, 2016.

INDEX

SHORT CUTS

INTRODUCTIONS TO FILM STUDIES